# The Professoriate Today

# The Professoriate Today

## Languishing in Dante's Purgatory

John Hampton

ROWMAN & LITTLEFIELD
*Lanham • Boulder • New York • London*

Published by Rowman & Littlefield International Ltd
Unit A, Whitacre Mews, 26-34 Stannary Street, London SE11 4AB
www.rowmaninternational.com

Rowman & Littlefield International Ltd.is an affiliate of Rowman & Littlefield
4501 Forbes Boulevard, Suite 200, Lanham, Maryland 20706, USA
With additional offices in Boulder, New York, Toronto (Canada), and Plymouth (UK)
www.rowman.com

Copyright © 2017 by John Hampton

*All rights reserved.* No part of this book may be reproduced in any form or by any electronic or mechanical means, including information storage and retrieval systems, without written permission from the publisher, except by a reviewer who may quote passages in a review.

**British Library Cataloguing in Publication Data**

A catalogue record for this book is available from the British Library

**Library of Congress Cataloging-in-Publication Data**

ISBN: 978-1-4758-3648-6 (cloth : alk. paper)
ISBN: 978-1-4758-3649-3 (pbk. : alk. paper)
ISBN: 978-1-4758-3650-9 (electronic)

∞™ The paper used in this publication meets the minimum requirements of American National Standard for Information Sciences—Permanence of Paper for Printed Library Materials, ANSI/NISO Z39.48-1992.

Printed in the United States of America

# Contents

Preface ix

Acknowledgments xiii

## PART I: WELCOME TO THE ACADEMY 1

1 What's All This Business about Purgatory? Do Professors Make a Stop Before They Reach Heaven? 3

2 Why Would Anybody in Their Right Mind Choose to Be a Professor? Would Electrical Shock Therapy Be a Better Choice? 11

3 Are Contingent Faculty the Barbarians at the Gate? What on Earth Is a Contingent Faculty? 19

4 What's the Buzz about Faculty Value over Replacement Economics? When Did This Silly Theory Creep In? 29

5 Are Tenured Professors an Endangered Species? Will the Last Full-time Professor Please Turn Out the Lights? 35

## PART II: WELCOME TO THE CLASSROOM 43

6 Who Do You Want in Front of the Classroom? Are Professors Perfect in Every Way? 45

7 Professor, Can You Ever Be Wrong? Do You Understand What Happens If You Don't Agree with Me? 59

8   Why Do Students Fail to Learn What I Fail to Teach? Why Did Nobody Tell Me Nothing about Teaching?    71

9   What Is Your Problem with Students Sleeping in Class? Would It Bother You if a Student Asked You to Keep It Down?    81

10  Did You Hear about the Death of Written Exams? Did the End of Cursive Writing Pass You By?    91

**PART III: LIFE ON THE FACULTY**    97

11  How about a Last Great Lecture Just for Posterity? Can You Offer Some Words of Wisdom for the Ages?    99

12  Should You Be David or Goliath in the Classroom? As Goliath Is My Role Model, What's the Question Here?    109

13  Is the Faculty Search Process Fatally Flawed? Why Do We Make so Many Wrong Hiring Decisions?    115

14  Is the Faculty Evaluation Process Fatally Flawed? What on Earth Is Going on in That Promotion and Tenure Committee?    127

15  Should You Do a Stint as Department Chair? Does Anybody Need This Grief?    137

**PART IV: PROTECTING WHAT WE HAVE**    147

16  Does a Liberal Arts Foundation Protect Anything That Needs Protecting? What Are We Teaching and Why Do We Teach It?    149

17  Does Anybody Believe in Hybrid and Distance-Learning Courses? Is a Changing World Your Friend or Your Enemy?    155

18  Does Academic Freedom Protect Anything That Needs Protecting? Would the Academy Collapse if Academic Freedom Went Away?    167

19  Does Tenure Protect Anything That Needs Protecting? Would the Academy Collapse if Tenure Went Away?    175

**PART V: CAREER DECISION-MAKING FOR PROFESSORS**    185

20  Despite It All, Would You Like to Be a Professor? Can You Tell Me More about Academic Purgatory?    187

| **21** | Can You Believe Limbo Is the Next Stop after Purgatory? Where, Oh Where, Is Tenure? | 195 |
| --- | --- | --- |
| **22** | Do You Know You Can Choose Your Own Limbo or Paradise? Does God Give Us so Many Options Simply Because She Loves Us? | 201 |

| Index | 209 |
| --- | --- |
| About the Author | 215 |

# Preface

Helping students can make anyone feel quite pleasant indeed. A father reported an engagement with his son when the boy was in high school. It captures the feeling some professors have quite often with their students.

*Son.* Father, I am having trouble in honors English. Mr. Gutherie is giving me C grades.

*Father.* That's not good.

*Son.* No. I did this paper that is due tomorrow. It's really good. Would you take a look at it?

*Father.* Sure.

*Son.* Thanks.

*Father.* I have a question. Do you want support for having done a good job or do you want help making it better?

*Son.* (Pause) I need help.

*Father.* OK, then.

At this point a question had the impact as though it asked, "Well son, now with your first sentence. Shouldn't it have both a subject and a verb?"

At that statement, the son almost burst into tears. Then he recovered, listened, and said "I got it."

Four days later, he walked into the kitchen with the words, "Got a hundred on Mr. Gutherie's paper. Thanks, Dad."

## DO YOU WANT HELP OR SUPPORT?

Many individuals who want to help young people are lured toward the life of a professor. Plus the prestige. Who wouldn't want to say the following at a cocktail party?

"Well, yes, I'm doing OK. I enjoy my job teaching at Princeton University. Being a full professor with tenure gives me a chance to do great things."

Some would-be scholars want support for their dreams. Others want advice. Let's be realistic. What does it mean to be a college professor?

## HISTORICAL ROLE OF THE ACADEMY

College is what it is and we cannot expect it to be more. Or can we? Professors motivate students to learn. Plato did it in the academy. His descendants did it in medieval and modern universities. Academic research has made colossal contributions to our civilization.

These statements do not fully capture the success of the academy. It lies in the unique interaction of the master and apprentice, the tutor and novice, the professor and student. It was true when Plato related his Allegory of the Cave.

A gathering of people sit chained in a cave facing a blank wall. The people watch shadows projected on the wall from things passing behind them. They give names to the shadows without ever seeing what created them.

For Plato, the student is the prisoner watching only shadows. The professor turns him around so he can see that which makes the shadow. In ancient Greece, enlightenment came from the philosopher in the academy. Since the Middle Ages, it has come from the professor.

## LIBERAL ARTS TRADITION

The academy of Plato morphed into a liberal arts education in a Judeo-Christian framework. Largely identified with Europe and North America, it is globally renowned for helping students understand the values, ethics, and ideas that created Western civilization. The liberal arts are grounded in philosophy and religion.

- Pre-Christian Concepts. Socrates (b. 470 BC), Plato, (b. 428 BC), and Aristotle (b. 384 BC).
- Early Christian Theologians. Paul of Tarsus (b. 5 BC), Augustine of Hippo (b. 354 AD), and Thomas Aquinas (b. 1225 AD).
- Renaissance Philosophers. Rene Descartes (b. 1596), John Locke (b. 1632), Isaac Newton (b. 1642), and Immanuel Kant (b. 1724).

Jesuit institutions augment the education with the teaching of Ignatius of Loyola (b. 1491).

## IS THERE A PROBLEM TODAY?

Do the Platonic and Renaissance methods still work? Of course they do. So what happened?

College is not what it used to be. The academy is no longer isolated from the external society. Some students go full-time to colleges where professors interact with them in small classes. Most do not.

Today's college is expected to serve many purposes. Society is unrealistic in its expectations of what it can do.

Finances come into play. Most students need help. How will they cover tuition? Are they borrowing too much?

Time pressures compound the anxiety. Students are advised to prepare for jobs after graduation and accept often-unpaid cooperative education and internship opportunities.

## HOW DOES THE PROFESSOR FIT IN?

The professor superseded the philosopher.

### Smart People Have PhDs

A PhD does not make you smart.

## DISCUSSION IN A CLASSROOM

A college professor was annoyed because one of his students was always late to class. One day the student sat down about fifteen minutes late. The following discussion ensued:

*Professor.* Mr. Harper. How many levels of deadly sin did Dante find on the mountain of purgatory?
*Student.* I don't know.
*Professor.* Perhaps if you came to class on time, you would know.
*Student.* That's not true. I never really pay attention.

## CUTTING TO THE CORE

The heart of the problem is an obsolete approach to learning. Curriculum management is often little more than ticking off required and disjointed courses. Lectures are often boring, written assignments tedious, and exams stressful.

## CHANGING CONDITION FOR PROFESSORS

Colleges and universities are under attack from many parties, including politicians, college administrators, parents, and students. The stakes for the professoriate are immense. Highly qualified teachers are migrant workers. Part-timers replace full-timers teaching large classes with little or no job security and low pay.

## PREMISE OF THIS BOOK

Considerable evidence exists that the most vocal discussions on higher education fail to understand what is happening. Stated simply:

A well-intentioned professoriate is out of step with reality and is slow to make changes desperately needed in higher education.

Escalator speech (thirty seconds)

> If you want to pursue a career as a professor, beware of the landscape you are about to enter. There are opportunities to do good things but there are also traps. This book focuses on the decisions that must be made to navigate the turbulent waters of the modern professoriate. Forearmed is forewarned.

Elevator speech (one minute)

> The changing role and expectations of higher education have reached a crisis point. The heart of the problem is an isolation of the professoriate. An emphasis on obscure research and lack of accountability is undermining the academy. Current approaches to writing a doctoral dissertation and pursuing tenure and promotion border on the absurd. They produce a period of suffering for new professors quite comparable to the description of purgatory in Dante's Divine Comedy. This book documents the story.

# Acknowledgments

Thanks to the many people—you know who you are—who contributed so unselfishly to the development of the stories in this book. God bless you all. A special thanks to Tracey Tango, who took time off from Tango Estate Sales to do the artwork, Professor Richard Ognibene, who provided counsel on key points of the manuscript, and Professor Mary Kate Naatus who inspires college students every single day.

John J. Hampton
Litchfield, CT
January 2017

# Part I
# WELCOME TO THE ACADEMY

*Chapter One*

# What's All This Business about Purgatory? Do Professors Make a Stop Before They Reach Heaven?

Abandon hope all ye who enter here.
—Dante Alighieri, Italian poet and politician

**BELIEVE IT OR NOT**

While working on his PhD at Stanford University, Theodore Streleski believed he was denied scholarly support by the professor directing his dissertation. He took a machinist's hammer and used it to beat his advisor to death. Shortly after the murder, he claimed it was a justifiable homicide based on the university's treatment of graduate students.

The murder occurred in 1978. Streleski was released in 1985. He spent nineteen years working on his degree while performing low-paying, part-time jobs. He spent seven years in jail.

**Question**
Did Mr. Streleski ever find a position as a full-time faculty member?

*Answer*
Apparently not. He was last seen in 1993 applying for a maintenance position with the San Francisco Municipal Railway. He was turned down for the job because of his crime.

**Question**

Does successfully completing a dissertation and finding a professorial appointment bring an end to anger about delays in finishing a PhD program?

*Answer*

Apparently not. There are many stories. In 1992, Valery Fabrikant, an engineering professor at Concordia University, killed four of his colleagues after blaming them for his failure to get tenure. After receiving a life sentence for murder, he settled down to do research from his prison cell. In 2002, he was quoted, "I ... had enough courage to fight lawlessness with deadly force and I hope to encourage others to do the same."

## STAGES OF LIFE

A human being goes through a process of birth, childhood, early maturity, later maturity, decline, and death. These stages have been studied and documented by scholars, philosophers, and others. We are keenly aware of the behaviors at different chronological ages and issues that affect happiness, sadness, anxiety, and satisfaction.

The exact same development applies to college professors or would-be professors. Birth precedes and death follows:

- **Early Maturity**. Matches graduate school.
- **Later Maturity**. Refers to becoming tenured and advancing in rank.
- **Decline**. Describes the aging process where research and teaching drop in quality.

## DANTE'S JOURNEY TO PARADISE

From this premise, we arrive at one of the great works of modern civilization. *The Divine Comedy* is a fourteenth-century epic poem by Dante Alighieri that describes his travels through hell, purgatory, and paradise. A professor's journey parallels the journey by Dante:

- **#1. Start of the Journey.** Dante begins in hell, allegorically a recognition of sin and the negative consequences of it. Professors may not be guilty of horrible sins, but something must happen that causes a person to consider spending his professional life outside the "real world." We can only speculate on this choice.

- **#2. Purgatory.** Here we can be more specific. Dante survived the depths of hell and reached purgatory, a temporary stopping point on the way to heaven. He climbed an allegorical mountain through the seven levels of deadly sins—pride, greed, lust, envy, gluttony, wrath, and sloth. It was a process of suffering and spiritual growth.
- **#3. Paradise.** Finally, Dante reaches a place where everyone can live in the perfect happiness and joy of the four cardinal virtues (prudence, justice, temperance, and fortitude) and the three theological virtues (faith, hope, and charity).

## Question
Why is Dante's poem identified as a comedy?

*Answer*
The term "comedy" had a different meaning in the Middle Ages. To Dante, as well as the ancient Greeks, it was the opposite of a tragedy. The comedy ended in a person's triumph while a tragedy ended in downfall or death. Today it is entertainment with a goal to make the audience laugh.

## Question
Is the choice to become a professor a comedy or a tragedy?

*Answer*
It can be either.

## PURGATORY

In Christian theology, purgatory is an intermediate state after physical death that people who are not quite yet ready to enter heaven go to. Sinners must atone for their misbehavior through a process of purification. The level of suffering varies from religion to religion but generally requires meeting specified beliefs or behavioral standards. After undergoing purification, they can achieve the holiness necessary to enter the joy of heaven. Living relatives and friends pray for them to leave purgatory and reach the heavenly gates without delay.

The concept of a temporary place of atonement has its roots in ancient cultures and religions. Christian texts picked it up in the twelfth century. Today it is used in a general sense to refer to any place or condition of suffering or torment, especially one that is temporary.

**Question**
Who prays for the success of a struggling dissertation candidate or an assistant professor who was rejected for tenure?

*Answer*
Maybe living relatives and friends?

## THE DEVIL IS IN THE DETAILS

Dante Alighieri's *The Divine Comedy* and John Milton's *Paradise Lost* are both classic stories that include descriptions of the devil. Dante was nothing if not creative in his portrayal of Satan, a giant demon with grotesque physical attributes. By contrast, Milton's Lucifer was the most beautiful of all angels prior to leading a rebellion against God and being expulsed from heaven.

The two poets also disagreed on the ambient temperature in hell. While Dante had it as a frozen land of ice and blizzard winds, Milton claimed it was a place of horrible fire.

The disagreement between the two epic poets continued on many levels. Milton, for example, explained the path as a choice among heaven, hell, or chaos. He had no purgatory at all.

**Question**
Should the absence of purgatory in *Paradise Lost* trouble us as we examine a possible purgatory in higher education?

*Answer*
Not at all. Synonyms for "chaos" include disorder, disarray, confusion, mayhem, and bedlam. From the perspective of a person suffering in purgatory, it may appear that chaos is ever present.

## PROFESSOR'S JOURNEY TO PARADISE

Generations of Americans have used college as a ticket to a better future. This can be measured in terms of a higher quality of life often, but not always accompanied by financial enrichment. Compared to individuals who cease education after high school, participation in a college experience once offered great social mobility, job security, and higher lifetime earnings. Today's students hope this continues to be true.

For some of these individuals, the path leads to a career in higher education. The most respected route leads to the status of "professor." Getting there can involve a long journey.

## ACADEMIC PURGATORY

In Dante's *Divine Comedy,* purgatory had seven levels. In the academy, we find a strikingly similar situation with five levels.

- **Graduate School.** To be a professor requires more than a college education. The individual must pursue much more knowledge to participate in a community of scholars. It usually consists of achieving a master's degree and doctoral coursework. The search for knowledge ends with a status recognized by the letters ABD (all but dissertation).
- **Dissertation.** After finishing coursework, the doctoral candidate displays the ability to perform and share research. She writes and defends a serious research inquiry in a specific field. A final document, identified either as a thesis or as a dissertation, is the output of this effort. If successful, a university confers a doctoral degree such as a PhD or EdD.
- **Full-time Position.** Once the degree is obtained, the newly minted graduate attempts to start a career in the academy. This involves finding faculty vacancies in the area of the degree, filling out applications, arranging interviews, receiving an offer, and accepting it.
- **Probation.** Once a faculty position has been obtained, the individual engages in teaching, scholarship, and service to prove worthy of being a lifelong member of the academy. This is often a maximum seven-year process in advance of tenure and promotion to associate professor.
- **Permanency.** This is a period of holding a secure and long-term position in an academic hierarchy. It normally starts as an associate professor with tenure and may include a promotion to full professor.

### Question
Is purgatory an accurate comparison for a person stuck on a dissertation or unable to obtain tenure and promotion?

*Answer*
Yes. In both cases, the situation is temporary. Finally, the successful individual may reach paradise in the form of a tenured professorship. However, some people will not make it. Not enough purification. They go to hell. What are you gonna do?

### Question
Under Dante's formulation, purgatory was not a voluntary assignment. People had no choice. Some went directly to hell. Others were good and obtained purification while still on earth. Heaven was their nonstop destination. Only

middle-of-the-road sinners went to purgatory. What is the situation for would-be professors?

*Answer*
Apparently most of them are sinners. Only a few rather famous scientists, politicians, and artists go directly to academic permanency.

**Question**
Do all professors finally reach heaven, which might be described as a promotion to full professor with tenure?

*Answer*
Unfortunately not. The end of purgatory can lead to heaven or hell. Some professors join the gods and live comfortably among the angels. Others find themselves in Dante's frozen wasteland or Milton's raging flames for a period of time that feels like eternity. Even with tenure, no promotion to full professor. No recognition of teaching skills or research.

## HELL AFTER PURGATORY

Dante warned us to abandon all hope when we enter hell. What will we find when we fail to be purified and are thrown to the devil? Professors in hell suffer from one or more recognizable emotional traumas:

- **Hatred for Students.** Occurs when students stop responding to their teaching, even when it is the professor's fault because he refuses to change or simply becomes bitter at the students' lack of motivation or interest in what he's saying.
- **Hatred for Administration.** Happens when the senior administrators display a pattern of conceit and superiority that they, no more talented than the average professor, make it out of the classroom and into a more exalted place.
- **Hatred for Colleagues.** Develops over time spent in worthless meetings with individuals who criticize everything in their environment including him personally.
- **Hatred for Teaching.** May develop quickly if he is not effective in the classroom and does not improve.
- **Hatred for Duties.** Ranges from department or committee meetings, registering students, or performing a series of mind-numbing tasks required by the administration, accreditors, or others.

## CONCLUSION

The journey into or through purgatory has been taken by hundreds of thousands of individuals in recent years. Many successful. Many not. In subsequent chapters, we will see the factors that determined success or failure and shaped opportunities and obstacles for individuals who have yet to take the journey or who are in the middle of it. Some of us may avoid purgatory completely and go directly through to the pearly academic gates.

All we can say is, "God bless them."

*Chapter Two*

# Why Would Anybody in Their Right Mind Choose to Be a Professor? Would Electrical Shock Therapy Be a Better Choice?

> Some people want it to happen, some wish it would happen, others make it happen.
>
> —Michael Jordan, basketball player

## WHAT IS A PROFESSOR?

The dictionary defines a professor as a teacher of the highest rank in a college or university. The title is not complete without recognizing three levels. Assistant professor is the entry level, even though the position does not actually "assist" anyone. Associate professor is the middle level, implying a status higher than helping others but not a full recognition. Professor, all by itself, is the top recognition.

For most individuals at the top rank, the term is not quite adequate. They often identify themselves as being "full" professors, lest anyone think they be mistaken for being in one of the lower categories. We will comply with the clarification throughout this book.

A separate category is the visiting professor, an individual of indeterminate rank invited to teach at a university or college for a limited period. The individual may be a professor from another institution, an individual of prominence in an academic discipline, or another notable and accomplished person such as an artist, writer, or politician. Individuals on such an appointment may alternatively be called a visiting scholar, researcher, fellow, or lecturer.

**Question**
Does everyone agree on the definition of the term "professor?"

*Answer*
Not really. Many academics think it applies only to full-time appointments at the rank of assistant, associate, or full professor. Not only that. The schools must be nonprofit as opposed to for-profit, offer tenure or other comparable long-term appointments after a probationary period, and expect professors to engage in teaching, scholarship, and service on a full-time basis.

## LOOKING BACK

Occasionally, we hear a senior professor lament, "If only I knew then what I know now." We hear this in the faculty lounge:

- I wish I knew not to waste so much time on my dissertation. I was not completing the definitive intellectual contribution in the subset of Hellenistic thought linking Sophism and Cynicism. I was just writing a G*damn paper to get a degree.
- Don't tell me to be grateful now. Tell the rank and tenure committee I deserved that promotion a long time ago.
- I wish I knew then how to resolve the conflict. My mother said, "Do what you love, not what you think you're supposed to do." The dean told me, "Publish your research in obscure journals in order to get promotion and tenure." Somewhere along the way I lost my love for creative writing.
- I thought he needed faculty support and I gave it. Why? Because I felt it was the right thing to do. If I knew then what I know now, I would have voted in favor of the resolution to censure the president.
- If you awake every morning with the thought that something wonderful will happen in your life today, you'll often find that you're right. Maybe I should have spent more time with my students and less time in the lab.

The academy provides considerable time for reflection. It can also be filled with relentless trivia involved with registering students, attending committee meetings, and participating in efforts to publish ideas that are of interest to no one. The trick is to get it right. Maybe this book can help.

## TOUGH START

Mainak Sarkar, thirty-eight years of age, was described by his high school teacher as calm, smart, and unassuming. "Mainak was a level-headed, intelligent student and never gave any indication of abnormal behavior." He graduated from one of India's elite engineering institutes where admission is fiercely competitive and students face huge pressure to excel.

The young man came to the United States to get his doctorate from UCLA. How did he do? Not well. He shot and killed his estranged wife in her suburban Minneapolis home, then drove 2,000 miles to California where he shot and killed his professor before taking his own life. Individuals who knew him in the United States speculated that he "may have been demoralized by the long struggle to earn his doctorate." A common problem. More than half of doctoral candidates never finish their dissertation.

## BUMP IN THE ROAD

Irwin Horwitz, a professor at Texas A&M at Galveston, told students he would fail everyone in his strategic management class. "Since teaching this course, I have caught cheating, been told to 'chill out,' 'get out of my space,' 'go back and teach,' and called a 'moron.'" He went on to say students cheated by signing in for one another, did not show up but claimed they did, and spread hurtful and untrue rumors about him.

Horwitz went on to say that none of the students deserve to pass the course or graduate from the university because they lack personal character, honor, maturity, and a willingness or competence to do quality work. He passed this message on to senior administrators of the university.

The university said that Horwitz's failing grades will not be upheld, even as the school would investigate the student behavior and take disciplinary action if appropriate.

Response to his actions were intense. Horwitz said he received and shared some e-mails that mocked him and others that praised him.

Asked if the decision was fair to every student, Horwitz said a few students showed good behavior and he would teach only them for the rest of the course. The university declined the offer and removed him from the class.

## WHO IS THIS GUY?

Eliot Spitzer served an eight-year term as Attorney General of New York before being elected governor, a post he held for a single year until a scandal linked him to an escort agency. A year after leaving office, he taught a political science course at the City College of New York.

Students reported he held classes for two and half hours with a ten-minute break and assigned hundreds of pages of readings every week. His style was characterized as being "demanding and wonkish, with a hefty dose of his two cents."

One student reported her reaction on the first night. "I just walked in and stopped and stared at him and was like, no way."

A reporter went to his class. Mr. Spitzer politely declined a request for the reporter to sit in. During the break, Eliot said many of his students had complimentary things to say about him. He continued, "It's only the second class. Wait until they get their midterms back."

## IS IT PRAISE TO BE CALLED WONKISH?

The student's choice of the word "Wonkish" is both interesting and troublesome. The word has multiple definitions. It can refer to a person who spends too much studying or writing and has little or no social life. More extreme, it describes a stupid, boring, or unattractive person. In higher education, we use it to describe professors who give excessive and nonstop attention to things that are totally unimportant.

Wonkish describes a behavior needed to complete a doctoral program and again to achieve tenure. Research is everything, let's be clear about that. The word is troublesome if it is not what you want in higher education. Maybe you also want people contact in a meaningful way.

### Question
All right. You would love to be a professor spending the day discussing the great works of Western civilization with eager students. You apply for admission to a great university. Cornell comes to mind. You think you can get in. Are you right?

### Answer
Maybe. In a recent year, Cornell accepted 22 students into the PhD program in English out of 258 applicants. You need to be in the lucky "9 percent." Be optimistic. At least you were not applying for a master of fine arts where Cornell accepted only 8 students out of 810 applicants.

## DON'T TAKE IT OUT ON THE MEDIA

A CBS MoneyWatch story recognized that many people believe earning a doctorate is the right start to a rewarding career. The television network ran a story that provided several reasons to take a second look.

The average PhD candidate takes more than eight years from start to finish. Newly minted doctors average thirty-three years of age when they apply for assistant professor positions, the lowest rank on the academic ladder. It may take many more years, or never, to actually get a position.

During candidacy years, professors will exploit you. The CBS piece pulled no punches pointing out:

> It takes forever to earn a doctorate degree because graduate students are routinely treated like slaves.

Harsh words to describe the grunt work that allows professors to publish research while delegating "distasteful" tasks. These include teaching undergraduates, grading papers, holding office hours, and "playing mother hen" to undergrads.

Some other considerations round out the story.

- You could fail to finish. Each year 850,000 applications are submitted for admission to doctoral programs. Twenty-two percent are accepted, about 140,000. Half as many graduate, few in under five years, eight years on average.
- You might end up on food stamps. This is the case for thirty thousand candidates, many of whom work as part-time professors. They usually earn less than the lowest paid full-time person on the campus.

## IS THERE A TIME LIMIT TO FINISH?

Martha Yablonsky began her PhD program in counseling education at Duquesne University in 2003. She finished the coursework in a few years and reached the all-but-dissertation (ABD) stage. During that time, she worked full time for Medicaid, part-time as a therapist doing mental health and other counseling, and part-time teaching at two area colleges.

She worked on her dissertation, continuing to pay tuition. When she started, her program had no limit to completion. She did not know that an eight-year time limit was added in 2004. Not to worry. If she had known, she might also know the university granted extensions if requested.

A representative of the Council of Graduate Schools observed that many universities setting a time limit to complete a doctoral degree is common. He also pointed out students are permitted to graduate under the rules in place at the time they enter a program.

Ms. Yablonsky received a notice in 2011 that her time ran out. She applied for a one-year extension and got it. She applied for another extension after demonstrating progress and the faculty approved it. The university overruled the faculty, possibly because of a bad relationship between faculty and administrators on the campus.

Ms. Yablonsky filed a lawsuit against Duquesne alleging breach of contract. It accused Duquesne of being "deceitful and inaccurate," claimed the denial was "arbitrary and mean-spirited," and suggested she was "an innocent victim of turf wars and petty bickering."

The story may or may not be over. In 2017, Martha Yablonsky's LinkedIn page shows her to be an active practicing therapist. Among her credentials, along with designations as a National Certified Counselor and Licensed Professional Counselor, is reference to an MSEd from Duquesne University.

## A CURSE DISGUISED AS A WISH?

Even now and then we see a phrase that has a dubious and even scary meaning. An example is "interesting times" as in the apparent wish, "May you live in interesting times." This is often attributed to China where the times were famines, disasters, and diseases that historically killed millions of people.

Another dubious wish is, "May you be recognized by people in high places." Perhaps the person conveying the request hopes you come to the attention of the Federal Bureau of Investigation or Internal Revenue Service.

A third benediction is, "May you get what you wish for." This could apply to an applicant to a doctoral program where 75 percent of those who start do not ever finish.

## TOLERATION IS NOT ENOUGH

Whenever we start on a journey, we know there can be difficult times. We sit back if we are riding and tolerate the boredom. We push through the pain if we are walking and deal with it. We hope somehow that reaching our destination will be worth all the misery.

**Question**
On the path to a doctoral degree, academic appointment, tenure, and promotion, should we be prepared to tolerate the adventure?

*Answer*
In most cases, it is not enough. You must learn how to love it. Find the colleagues who share your love of teaching or research. Enjoy the students because of their weaknesses as well as talents. Feel sorry for the administrators who perform trivial tasks in poorly managed environments.

## CONCLUSION

From the perspective of "Love it, don't tolerate it," we find the professoriate can be the right choice for people. Not any easy road in all cases but neither are we staying one place. A reminder though, "Many are called, but few are chosen." This biblical line from Matthew 22:14 refers to a wedding feast. Perhaps the message should be heeded before starting the painstaking journey into the academy.

*Chapter Three*

# Are Contingent Faculty the Barbarians at the Gate? What on Earth Is a Contingent Faculty?

I was either still dreaming or I had entered an alternate reality where I was a flippin' insane person.

—Peggy Martinez, author

**Question**
A tenured professor at a cocktail party struck up a conversation with another guest.

*Professor:* So what do you do?

*Guest:* I'm a professor, too.

*Professor:* Where do you teach?

*Guest:* On Monday, Wednesday, and Friday morning I teach two courses at Florida International University. On Tuesday and Thursday, two more classes at Miami Dade Community. Tuesday evenings at Lindsey Hopkins, and Wednesday evenings at Nova Southeastern.

*Professor:* Are any of the positions full-time?

*Guest:* Not yet.

*Professor:* Nice talking to you. See you later.

What just happened?

*Answer*
We witnessed a chance encounter between a professor and a contingent faculty member. Such events also occur occasionally and briefly in the hallways at colleges and universities.

## Question

Emily Van Duyne was a part-time instructor whose teaching load peaked at the equivalent of sixteen courses a year. She described what it was like to go from adjunct to tenure-track faculty at Stockton State College. Did her life improve?

*Answer*

Yes. Emily pointed out a fact of academic life. The difference between being adjunct and full-time can't be overstated. Some quotes:

- "Lovely in that I got what I so badly." She no longer felt like a fraud when she called herself a professor.
- "Disturbing." It proved feelings and theories she had about her previous low status as an adjunct.
- "All of the sudden, people saw me." Previously she was invisible.
- "More than that, they listened to me." People asked her questions and believed she had authority.
- "I have institutional support." She was given funds to travel to conferences and do research.

## THE MEDIEVAL GUILD

A guild was an association of artisans or merchants that rose to prominence in the Middle Ages in Europe. The defining characteristic was it controlled the practice of a craft in a particular town. It mixed the characteristics of a trade union, cartel, and secret society. It had the power from a monarch, emperor, or prince to control the destiny of its members. It could exclude from the profession nonmembers or members who did not comply with guidelines.

A guild had two categories of members and one category of hopefuls:

- **Master Craftsman.** An experienced and confirmed expert in a field of endeavor.
- **Journeyman.** An individual learning the skills needed to become a master craftsman.
- **Apprentice.** An individual learning basic skills while being evaluated for possible membership. The most cherished secrets of the guild were not shared with them.

An apprentice who showed promise would advance to journeyman. During this probationary period, he would produce a masterpiece and present it to the masters. If it was not accepted, he would remain a journeyman, possibly for the rest of his life.

## The Medieval University

In the twelfth century, the guild concept was applied to universities such as Oxford, Paris, and Bologna. Guilds share their tools and materials only with their members. This practice was followed by universities where books and tutorials were the tools of understanding science, natural phenomenon, religion, and technology.

Universities initially did not have separate facilities. Rather, groups of learned individuals called masters conducted sessions in churches, community centers, and homes. They were financed, which meant paying the teachers, following three models. The king paid the teachers at Oxford. The Catholic Church paid the teachers in Paris. The students paid the teachers in Bologna.

The holder of the academic degree of master of arts was the top dog in the "academic guild." The other teachers were the journeymen. The students filled the role of apprentice. The teachers moved around as many of the "masters" were highly sought. Kings, princes, and clergy fought for them as they built the prestige and reputation of their various "universitas."

Higher education took a major step in a new direction in Germany in the nineteenth century with a degree to supersede the master's level. The research doctorate was born in concept and slowly took hold. The "masterpiece" of the original guilds resurfaced as the dissertation, a crowning achievement of years of academic preparation. It received its fullest manifestation in the degree of doctor of philosophy, or PhD, even as it expanded to other titles and letters.

Early in the twentieth century the PhD became the standard degree for a permanent university appointment with the title of professor. If an individual joined the academy without a master's degree, the university gave the person the status of apprentice. A master's degree identified a journeyman. In this capacity, the individual had to obtain a PhD to advance further.

Two "masterpieces" would be required to reach the top.

- **Dissertation.** This was the crowning achievement of the apprentice period. It was proof that the individual had the capabilities to conduct research and develop into a senior scholar.
- **Acceptance by Peers.** This was dissemination of research beyond the dissertation and recognition of it by peers across the range of knowledge of a discipline.

Thus, we have "publish or perish."

## Publish or Perish

Modern universities modified the masterpiece in the history of guilds. It became the dissertation awarded at the end of the apprenticeship when the newly minted PhD is advanced to "guild" membership at the rank of assistant professor. The "journeyman" enters a seven-year probationary period to achieve the status of associate professor, the lower rank of the original "master" designation. Success comes when the individual produces new research, submits it to his peers for evaluation, and they approve of it.

The second approval is critical. In ancient guilds, journeymen could continue to practice, albeit at the less prestigious level. Not the case in the academy. It was up or out.

Going up was good as it was accompanied by a virtual lifetime guarantee of employment. The mechanism was tenure and everybody agreed not to touch its permanency. Failing to achieve it was bad. No appeal. No recourse. Goodbye.

## THE MODERN ACADEMIC GUILD

We can take a detour at this point. The American Association of University Professors (AAUP) is, for all practical purposes, the modern guild of the academy. It is a rather fine professional association of professors and academic administrators that guards the covenant of the teaching profession.

The AAUP has been engaged in an uphill battle for many years to preserve the rights of the professoriate. It participated in some battles and watched from the sidelines in others. Today, the academy of Plato is hardly recognizable in most areas of U.S. higher education. Perhaps the biggest change is examined in an AAUP position paper titled, "Background Facts on Contingent Faculty."

We might start the discussion with "full-time faculty." What does that mean?

## Full-time Faculty

We have no widely accepted definition of the term "full time" when discussing faculty positions in higher education. The accreditors do not define it and neither do most colleges. They just use it in their academic handbooks, guidelines, and policies.

The Fair Labor Standards Act does not help. It accepts each employer's definition of full-time or part-time. Commonly this means thirty-five to forty working hours per week. State governments tend to use thirty-five hours. Airlines define it for pilots as seventy-five to ninety flight hours per month. An accounting firm during tax season may define work week as 8:00 am to

8:00 pm Monday to Thursday and 8:00 am to 5:00 pm Friday and Saturday, a weekly total of fifty-six hours. Salaried employees may have no definition at all in terms of hours worked.

Higher education faces a unique problem in defining full time. An instructor may be in class for twelve to fifteen hours per week and be required to maintain three hours for student advising. No time is prescribed for preparing for class, grading exams, reading papers, reporting grades, or performing other necessary tasks.

**Question**
Professor "A" teaches four courses during each of the fall and spring semesters. Professor "B" teaches six classes in the fall and five classes in the spring. Are they both full-time faculty members?

*Answer*
We cannot tell from the information given. Part-time faculty members are paid per course and can accept any number of assignments. The only way to know that a person has full-time status is for the term to be used in the letter of appointment or the academic or faculty handbook.

**Contingent Faculty**

This refers to either part- and full-time nontenure-track faculty. Perhaps the biggest nightmare for would-be professors arises from this simple two-word phrase.

The term "contingent faculty" is curious to say the least. Here are the thesaurus synonyms that could be describing these teachers:

- **Chance.** They arrive in the absence of any obvious design.
- **Accidental.** Their appointment happens unexpectedly.
- **Fortuitous.** They exist as a lucky chance of fate.
- **Possible.** They enter the classroom as a result of the power of some unknown person.
- **Unforeseeable.** We do not know who will show up if anyone.
- **Unpredictable.** We are unable to anticipate or know if they will arrive on time or at all.
- **Random.** They may show up at the wrong time or place.
- **Haphazard.** We have no idea what they will do after they arrive.

Which one should we choose? It doesn't matter if we simply point out the distinguishing characteristic of the category. Colleges and universities make little or no long-term commitment to the individuals.

The status often hides under appointments with titles such as adjunct, lecturer, or faculty associate. It can also apply to graduate assistant and part-time instructor, even as these individuals may teach the equivalent of or more than a full-time course load.

An explicit condition of employment in most academic environments is that this cohort of faculty cannot receive tenure and is not eligible for many benefits of "professors" in the academy. Plus, they can be released with little formal effort simply by not renewing their semester, annual, or other short-term contracts.

## *Compensation for Contingent Faculty*

The AAUP is quite specific on paying and supporting part-timers and nontenure-track faculty. From its position paper:

> The excessive use of, and inadequate compensation and professional support for, contingent faculty exploits these colleagues. Positions that require comparable work, responsibilities, and qualifications should be comparably compensated.

**Question**
The AAUP supports paying part-timers the "applicable fraction" of the compensation of full-timers. What does this mean?

*Answer*
If a professor earns $80,000 for teaching eight courses a year, the part-timer teaching one course should receive one-eighth or $10,000.

The AAUP points out that colleges pay part-timers less as a conscious economic decision rather than a matter of economic necessity. Acknowledging budget cuts, the practice grew dramatically during times of economic prosperity. Colleges invested heavily in facilities and technology while cutting instructional spending.

**The Meaning.** Incoming students may find finer facilities but also fewer full-time faculty with adequate time to mentor them.

## *The Case against Contingent Faculty*

It is hard to dispute the AAUP concerns about treatment of contingent faculty. While acknowledging that many of them are excellent teachers and scholars, they lack access to resources including offices, computer support, and maybe even photocopying services. Consequently, the AAUP concludes, "Heavy reliance on contingent faculty hurts students." Let's evaluate that statement.

**Concern #1.** Contingent faculty are typically paid only for the hours they spend in the classroom.

**Evaluation.** The same is true for tenured faculty who often have a research priority. Untenured faculty particularly must pay attention to publishing.

**Concern #2.** Contingent faculty are often hired on the spur of the moment with little evaluation.

**Evaluation.** This may be offset by a reality that they are hired primarily to teach, not conduct research. Many observers believe adjunct faculty members do a better job in the classroom than tenured or tenure-track professors.

**Concern #3.** The high turnover among contingent faculty members means some students may never have the same teacher twice.

**Evaluation.** This has positive and negative outcomes. Students can be hurt if multiple required courses are taught only by a single professor.

**Concern #4.** Students may not be able to find instructors who know them well enough to write letters of recommendation.

**Evaluation.** This may or may not be true since many part-timers teach lower-level general curriculum courses while recommendations tend to be needed from professors in upper-level major courses.

**Concern #5.** Overuse of contingent faculty hurts the integrity of faculty work as tasks are divided and assigned piecemeal to instructors, lecturers, graduate students, specialists, researchers, and administrators.

**Evaluation.** The accusations of harm also include the advising of students, setting curriculum, and service on college-wide committees. This is a curious concern with no easy way to verify it.

*AAUP Conclusion on Contingent Faculty*

The AAUP makes specific recommendations:

- Use of nontenure-track appointments should be limited to specialized fields and emergency situations.
- No more than 15 to 25 percent of instruction should be provided by nontenure-track faculty.
- Shared governance responsibilities should be shared among all faculty, including part-timers.
- Contingent faculty should have job security and due process protections.

## Stakeholder Views on Contingent Faculty

Everybody knows the AAUP view on contingent faculty. What is the view of some others? Let's make a guess.

- **Department Chair and Dean.** Probably agree with the AAUP but for different reasons. It's a pain in the neck to hire six to eight adjuncts to cover the courses assigned to a single professor. Let's hire one person, assign him or her to the same basic courses every year, and be done with it.
- **Academic and other Vice Presidents.** They don't care either, except maybe the finance VP who is trying to save a buck and any other VPs who hope hiring part-timers will free up more funds for athletics, computers, or something else.
- **The President or Trustees.** They do not care. That's not what they do or why they took their positions.
- **Students.** They may prefer part-timers who are interested in teaching rather than tenured or tenure-track professors who care mostly about research.
- **Parents and Politicians.** They think it is horrible that part-timers teach their children and constituents. They do not know the issues and would not be that interested in them if they did. They just want a school with a good reputation. The other stuff does not matter if nobody brings it up.

## TENURED AND TENURE-TRACK FACULTY VIEWS

All that's left for us to do is think about everybody's view of the quality of learning. Do they carry the teaching workload or sluff off? This is a mixed bag.

- **Tenured Professor, Superstar.** Does not care. Too busy to bother with peripheral issues, students, or colleagues who are being trampled in the dust.
- **Tenured Professor, Struggling to Stay Relevant.** Not his or her issue. A lot of other things to do.
- **Tenured Professor, Inactive Researcher.** May be interested in teaching. May be not. Definitely not interested in the problems of contingent faculty.
- **Tenured Associate Professor Seeking Promotion.** Worried about campus politics. Does not need to offend tenured professors or the dean. Not interested.
- **Tenured Lifetime Associate Professor.** Has given up the fight or has nothing left to do but fight. Could go either way.
- **Tenure-track Assistant Professor.** Keep your head down, write and submit articles to journals, get tenure and promotion. Not your issue.

- **Contingent Faculty.** A living nightmare for those seeking a career in the academy. Got to get out of the trap. Anxiety and stress. Thank God for selective serotonin reuptake inhibitors (SSRIs) such as Lexapro, Luvox, Paxil, Prozac, and Zoloft.

## CONTINGENT FACULTY AT THE GATE

The term "barbarian" refers to a person from another nation or group deemed to have a primitive civilization. More harshly, it is a fierce, brutal, or cruel person who wants to harm us. Barbarians at the gate in Roman times were uneducated people trying to climb over a wall that kept them from destroying our civilization.

Many members of the academy see contingent faculty members as individuals who will damage the professoriate. They are primitive in the sense that they lack doctoral degrees and research ambitions. Their behavior threatens the enlightenment that is found with in the academic compound.

Is this true? Is this reasonable? We will return to these questions in upcoming chapters.

## CONCLUSION

Whatever else we conclude on the issue of contingent faculty, we might recognize that the situation produces instability, confusion, and anger. It is part of the reality that members of the academy are languishing in purgatory.

*Chapter Four*

# What's the Buzz about Faculty Value over Replacement Economics? When Did This Silly Theory Creep In?

> The juvenile sea squirt wanders through the sea searching for ... its home for life ... When it finds its spot ... it doesn't need its brain anymore, so it eats it! It's rather like getting tenure.
>
> —Daniel C. Dennett, American philosopher

## THE DISMAL SCIENCE

At the turn of the eighteenth century, Robert Malthus argued that unchecked population growth would eventually doom the world to widespread starvation. The fear led to political and social movements including Thomas Carlyle's coining the term "dismal science" to refer to the economics of shortages. It took more than a hundred years for the concept to reach higher education.

## ADMINISTRATION VIEW ON FACULTY DUTIES

College presidents and deans often take a Malthusian perspective on tenured faculty when budgets get tight, or even when they don't, college administrators reflect upon the state of the permanent faculty.

The process often starts with identifying the things faculty members are expected to do.

- **Teach Courses.** Time in front of students or working on distance learning.
- **Support Teaching.** Prepare lectures, syllabi, and exams and meet with students outside class.
- **Support Students.** Advise on courses, careers, and write recommendations for employment and graduate school.
- **Do Research.** Collect data, develop findings, present them at scholarly conferences, and publish them.
- **Maintain Knowledge.** Read scholarly journals to keep up-to-date in one's field of study.
- **Do Other Service.** Join campus committees and scholarly societies and edit academic journals.
- **Attend Ceremonies.** Participate in graduation, convocations, and awards presentations.

**Question**
What do administrators do with the list once they have it?

*Answer*
Some accept it as the traditional role of "masters" in the academy. Others fret. Why pay so much money for tasks that are not important to the college mission?

## ASSESSING NEED FOR FACULTY

Administrators often ask, "What do we need from the faculty?" They identify the following:

- **Valuable Activities.** Teach courses and support students with advising.
- **Useful Activities.** Attend occasional ceremonies. Enhance the school reputation with research and writing. Serve on committees.
- **Hobbies.** Stay current in their teaching area and engage in community, professional, and off campus service.

The assessment can lead to an economic analysis. Why pay for things we don't need? This highlights the ratio of permanent and contingent instructors. Teaching duties? Nonteaching duties? How many full-timers do we need? The tension has led to an increasing number of lower-cost contingency faculty with full-time workloads with lower salaries and benefits.

## BASEBALL ECONOMICS

Value over Replacement Player (VORP) economics is used in professional baseball to compare how much value one player brings compared to other available individuals. Many colleges seem to be using the same kind of analysis.

As an example, a college has a need for instructors to teach twenty-four classes in a year. A full-timer teaches eight courses annually and would cost $60,000 in salary and benefits. A part-timer would receive $4,000 per course. The cost comparisons are as follows:

|              | *Full-timers* | *Part-timers* |
|--------------|---------------|---------------|
| Number       | 3             | 24            |
| Cost of each | $60,000       | $4,000        |
| Total        | $180,000      | $96,000       |
| VORP         |               | **$84,000**   |

If the dean replaces three professors with twenty-four adjuncts, she saves $84,000. That's step number one.

Next, she considers value added by full-timers. If they are not available to advise students, the dean may need to hire an advisor. If they are not available to participate on curriculum and academic standards committees or attend open houses for incoming students, what will be the impact?

Finally, she decides. Maybe she hires two full-timers and eight part-timers.

**Question**
What does VORP economics tell the administrators who use it?

*Answer*
Contingent faculty are a good deal. They perform the valuable tasks of teaching. They can attend ceremonies and contribute to an occasional school project if needed. The school does not have to pay for their less valuable service and "hobbies."

**Question**
Wait a minute. What about the research that helps a university build its reputation?

*Answer*
OK. Maybe a few research-oriented professors, sprinkled with a superstar if we can afford it, will fix this issue.

**Question**

Many schools only reimburse the cost of attending conferences if a professor is a speaker or panel member. An instructor has an acceptance to present as part of a panel at a conference where 96 percent of submitted papers are accepted for presentation. How many professors will hear the presentation?

*Answer*

It is not uncommon that the session will have an audience consisting of a panel moderator, four panel members, and seven to twelve attendees.

## An Offset to VORP Economics

One remaining viewpoint comes from faculty duties outside of teaching, advising, and research. What role do full-time faculty members play in the leadership and management of the college or university? Do they contribute to better management, improved learning, or better interpersonal outcomes for students, staff, and other stakeholders?

The AAUP thinks so and may be right. On the other hand, service on the campus is filled with unnecessary or trivial meetings and activities that have no impact on learning or anything else.

Table 4.1 shows the list of faculty committees in 2016 for a single liberal arts college with a full-time faculty of 114 lecturers and professors. You can make your own judgment on the value of the output of the committees on the list.

## How Do Deans Assess Faculty?

The economic view of contingent faculty may not carry over to the academic side of the house. Deans, administrators by title, are usually academics at heart. They prefer full-time "masters."

## How Do Peers Assess Colleagues?

The president of the university makes the decision on faculty hiring, retention, and promotion. Well, that's the strange part of the academy. Professors think they make it.

The university establishes search and promotion and tenure (P&T) processes. Typically, tenured professors and deans make recommendations. The president or board makes the final decision.

Although this process is clearly explained in academic handbooks, most professors do not believe it. If a president fails to take a faculty recommendation, it becomes a major scandal.

**Table 4.1  List of College Committees**

Academic Council, Day School Committee
Academic Council, Evening School Committee
Academic Standards Committee
Athletics Committee
Calendar Committee
Curriculum Committee
Development Committee
Enrollment Committee
Enrollment Council Committee
Experiential Learning–Service Learning Committee
Faculty Administration Grievance Board Committee
Faculty Hearing Board Committee
Faculty Rights and Responsibilities Committee
Graduate Programs Committee
Honors Program Committee
Inclusion, Diversity, Equity, and Access Committee
Library Committee
Nominations Committee
Personnel Welfare Committee
Pluralism Committee
Pluralism Courses Committee
Professional Development of the Faculty Committee
Rank & Tenure Committee
Speakers & Expression Committee
Strategic Planning and Budget Committee
Student Affairs Committee
Student Grievance Board Committee
Student Learning Outcomes Assessment Committee
University Services Committee
Value Courses Committee
Writing Intensive Courses Committee

# CONCLUSION

The role of contingent faculty generates considerable heat and smoke, as well it should. The value of higher education is the reality that it advances society. Economic and noneconomic forces produce tensions that must be addressed as part of educational reform. Our failure to address them to date leaves many members of the professoriate stuck in a purgatory that is not of their own making.

*Chapter Five*

# Are Tenured Professors an Endangered Species? Will the Last Full-time Professor Please Turn Out the Lights?

We all have a responsibility to protect endangered species, both for their sake and for the sake of our own future generations.

—Loretta Lynch, U.S. Attorney General

### PART-TIMERS IN THE HALLWAYS

Today, more than 70 percent of all college courses are taught by part-time faculty. They teach basic core courses, not those that are more advanced and interesting. They may commute between two or more institutions, prepare courses on short-term notice, and make enormous sacrifices to interact with students. They often lack health care and retirement benefits even as they pay all applicable taxes.

Many contingent faculty do not have professional careers outside teaching. An exception are specialists or practitioners of a profession, such as law or architecture, who teach a class on the side. These individuals represent a small portion of the teaching faculty.

### INCIDENT AT CHAFFEY COLLEGE

In 2013, a professor was fired two weeks before the final exam at Chaffey College in California. A dean delivered the news without further explanation. When asked by a reporter, the College refused to comment on the matter. The instructor, Stefan Veldhuis, told the reporter a school administrator simply phoned him and told him he was no longer a "good fit."

The action occurred after Veldhuis reported that another college employee was having sex in a classroom. Veldhuis speculated that employee might have retaliated by falsely accusing Veldhuis of something.

**Question**
Maybe the school suddenly found out professor Veldhuis was not qualified to teach college courses. Is that likely?

*Answer*
No. He has a master's degree and had taught at the college for eight years. In the fiscal year prior to the termination, he earned a reported $34,000 teaching as an adjunct. That likely means he taught ten to twelve courses.

**Question**
Maybe the students finally got fed up with his bad teaching and protested. Did that occur?

*Answer*
No. He was a popular instructor as reflected in a 4.8 out of 5 rating on the Rate My Professor website. After the firing was announced, many of his students complained to the college, even setting up a support page for him on Facebook.

**Question**
So what can explain terminating a professor with no real explanation a few weeks before the end of a semester?

*Answer*
Perhaps a serious or deplorable incident occurred that cannot be reported to the public. The college deserves the benefit of the doubt. The story does illustrate the lack of due process when colleges deal with adjunct teachers.

## SWIMMING AGAINST THE CURRENT

A professor uses an example of approaching a river to encourage critical and creative thinking. He asks the class what they would do and why they would do it. After some discussion, they link their decisions to the reason they arrived on the riverbank.

- If they want to go somewhere, they swim downstream.

- If they want exercise, they swim upstream.
- If they want to cross it, they look for a bridge.

We might encourage people to perform a similar exercise when considering a career in higher education. Suppose you have a master's degree. As you stand on the riverbank, you look at the academy on the far shore. Should you enter the water or find a bridge? Without a doctorate, there are two possibilities:

- **Swim Upstream.** This effort will take you nowhere. The current is too strong.
- **Swim Downstream.** Now you find yourself moving but it is not in the direction you want. Each stroke will take you further away from your goal.

What should you do? Find a bridge. It's right there. Start and complete a doctoral degree that requires a dissertation. It will lift you across to the other shore. But a caveat. Passage using the bridge is not free. You must be willing and able to pay the toll.

## FIRST LEVEL OF ACADEMIC PURGATORY

Enough with the river. Let's cross the bridge. The good news is you can pay a small toll and start to cross. The bad news is a separate toll is collected constantly as you proceed. The highest cost, in both emotional and physical terms, occurs after all courses and exams are completed. The candidate reaches the all-but-dissertation (ABD) stage. Get ready to dig down deep to pay successive tools.

To gain a metaphorical view of what happens, we can look to the following movie:

> *The Trench.* (Distributed by the Arts Council of England. Release date: 1999. Running time: ninety-eight minutes. Language: English)
> The film paints a picture of the soldiers' emotional experience in the confines of the trenches in World War I; an experience running the gamut from boredom to fear and panic.

## TIME TO DEGREE COMPLETION

Once in the trench, how long do you stay there? The answer varies by discipline. Some averages from start to completion:

| Discipline | Time to Completion (years) |
|---|---|
| Physical Sciences | 6 |
| Engineering | 6 |
| Life Sciences | 7 |
| Social Sciences | 8 |
| Humanities | 9 |
| Education | 11 |

## OBSTACLES TO DEGREE COMPLETION

Life in the ABD trench has unexpected obstacles to survival:

- **Dissertation Director.** This professor may be supportive, helpful, missing in action, incompetent, lazy, or micromanagerial. Although required to eventually approve the dissertation, she may procrastinate, fail to communicate, change schools, retire, or die. Many candidates hope for death.
- **Health of the Candidate.** The project grows formidable over time. It starts like a marathon of 26 miles (42 km). Then it becomes an Ironman Triathlon consisting of a 2.4-mile (4 km) swim, a 112-mile (180 km) bicycle ride, and then a 26-mile run. No amount of training can prepare you for it.
- **Misunderstanding by the Candidate.** At the start of the ABD stage, the candidate believes he will write the definitive study in an area of discipline. His research will produce fame and success. The reality is no one is interested in it and no one will publish it.
- **Despair by the Candidate.** At some point, progress slows to a crawl. It may occur when searching prior research turns into running around in circles dealing with the director. The tension may annoy the director who now does less to help.

## DOWNHILL ABD SLOPE

The dissertation effort often leads to psychological deterioration.

- **Review of the Literature.** The candidate believes she must identify every shred of pre-existing scholarship. The review of the literature never ends.
- **Procrastination.** After submitting drafts of proposals, research models, and details of the project, the advisor provides conflicting, obtuse, and even absurd comments after a lengthy and unexplained delay. The real problem is probably a total lack of interest by the director. Whatever the reason, the candidate stops making progress.

- **Embarrassment.** Family, friends, colleagues, and other ask, "So how are you doing?" As time passes, it is increasingly difficult to explain the gap between completing coursework and completion of the degree.
- **Paralysis.** At this point the project is stalled at best and dead at worst.

As time passes, the effort either succeeds or fails.

### Question
Some people think a downhill spiral is not the most apt description of writing a dissertation. Is there a more accurate allegory for the process?

*Answer*
How about Homer's ancient Greek story of Sisyphus? The gods condemned him to ceaselessly try to roll a rock to the top of a mountain. After substantial pain and effort, the stone would fall back under its own weight. For too many candidates, the dissertation is nothing more than a futile and hopeless labor.

## FINISHING THE DISSERTATION

Given all these obstacles, what do you do? Focus yourself.

- Select a director that you know and like and who likes you. Offer to help with her research agenda. Do anything so the director feels motivated to help you.
- Complete a competent review of the literature, forty to sixty pages or so, and stop. Write down what you find in the prescribed format. Lock down the chapter. Do not touch it again. If someone demands that you add something, do it and lock it down again.
- Design the methodology and start doing the research. Check off the boxes in the process, normally a series of obsessive and trivial roadblocks. Dot the *i*s, cross the *t*s, and stay the course.
- Write, write, write. It does not have to be perfect. Most directors will stop reading it if you have volume.

### Question
Can we view the dissertation approval as something of a game?

*Answer*
Yes. Dissertation writing is akin to Whac-a-Mole. Each of the five holes on the table contains a single plastic mole that randomly pops up. Hit it on the head so it goes back into the hole and you score points. The quicker you do

Table 5.1  Tuition/Fees in Selected Doctoral Programs

| School | Tuition/Fees ($) |
|---|---|
| Barry | 36,000+ |
| Capella | 56,000+ |
| Case Western (DM program) | 150,000+ |
| Duke | 58,000+ |
| Pace (DPS program) | 70,000+ |
| Rutgers (in-state) | 18,000+ |
| Rutgers (out-of-state) | 30,000+ |
| UCLA (in-state) | 16,000+ |
| UCLA (out-of-state) | 32,000+ |
| Walden | 60,000+ |

it, the higher your score. The prize for winning the game is a credential that allows you to be a professor.

## HOW EXPENSIVE IS A PHD?

The cost of a PhD program consists of components:

- **Direct Costs.** Tuition and fees continue over the time between initial enrollment and completion. See table 5.1.
- **Incidental Costs.** Additional expenses such as travel and lodging may be needed to participate in a program.
- **Financing Costs.** Interest is paid on borrowed money. Almost half of PhD candidates borrow with a median debt of $40,000 by the end.
- **Loss of Income**. Loss of wages or salary may occur if a break in employment costs a loss of seniority raises and reduced cumulative lifetime earnings.

## POST-PHD JOB MARKET

It may be expensive but more than fifty thousand people complete the journey to the PhD. What now? How many gain jobs in the academy? Recent statistics shows three times as many new PhDs as vacant full-time faculty openings. Even more distressing is the fact that half of all candidates who start a PhD program fail to complete it in ten years. Of those who finish, only a quarter of them land a full-time appointment within five years of graduating.

| | |
|---|---|
| New Doctoral Candidates | 100,000 |
| Doctoral Degrees Awarded | 52,000 |
| Vacant Academic Positions | 15,000 |

## SUCCESS ACHIEVING TENURE

The stark fact of life is that many successful PhD candidates will not get tenure or multiyear renewable contracts. Once upon a time, most professors who played the game ultimately secured lifetime employment, at least until age sixty-five. Or did they? A late 1990s survey of individuals who completed doctoral programs ten years earlier found two-thirds had positions in the academy and slightly more than half of them had tenure. The numbers varied by discipline.

| Discipline | Tenured (percent) |
|---|---|
| **Percentage in the Academy Ten Years After PhD Awarded (1998)** | |
| Sciences | 47 |
| Engineering | 40 |
| Computer Science | 57 |
| Humanities | 73 |
| Mathematics | 76 |
| **Percentage Tenured Ten Years after PhD Awarded (1998)** | |
| Sciences | 25 |
| Engineering | 36 |
| Computer Science | 48 |
| Humanities | 60 |
| Mathematics | 64 |

Things have changed. Nontenure-track position now makes up more than two-thirds of all faculty openings. Many soon-to-be graduates will not find academic jobs waiting for them.

### Question
The following question was posted on a higher education discussion website.

> I am a tenured associate professor in a very toxic department where the climate and interaction have been getting worse for years. Now, we hear rumors that the university may close the department and release the faculty. I researched Internet jobs. According to data in the Chronicle of Higher Education, the salaries are low. What should I do?

*Answer*
Responses presented a variety of viewpoints.

- "Apply for low-paying positions recognizing factors such as inaccurate published salary data."
- "Frame yourself as a unique situation and explain you would need more money."
- "Apply, then negotiate after receiving an offer."
- "Apply to everything. Universities prefer to fill positions with lower-priced assistant professors or lecturers. Don't wait a minute."

## CONCLUSION

Are full-time faculty an endangered species? The evidence is not that extreme. With more than 4,000 colleges and 1.5 million college teachers in the United States and Canada, we can expect a need for teachers in future years. With more than half of current positions filled with adjuncts, and the trend continuing to replace full-time with part-time instructors, the path to a permanent professorship is perilous indeed. Some will succeed and many will not.

*Part II*

# WELCOME TO THE CLASSROOM

*Chapter Six*

# Who Do You Want in Front of the Classroom? Are Professors Perfect in Every Way?

> When you study great teachers ... you will learn much more from their caring and hard work than from their style.
>
> —William Glasser, psychiatrist and interventionist

### BELIEVE IT OR NOT

An executive in residence program invites prominent successful people to share stories with students and alumni. If they are given a choice from among the following speakers, which one do you think they would prefer?

- **Tim Parks**. British novelist and translator. Author of sixteen novels, nine nonfiction books, sixteen translations of books from Italian into English, and hundreds of monographs. Two novels nominated for one of the most prestigious prizes in literature. Associate professor at a prestigious university.
- **Donald Trump.** American businessman, television personality, author, and politician. Real-estate ventures and other business interests. Elected president of the United States in 2016. Bachelor's degree from the Wharton School of the University of Pennsylvania.
- **Tiger Woods.** American professional golfer. Won more major golf tournaments than any golfer in history. Dropped out after two years at Stanford University.

- **Captain Richard Phillips.** Master of the *Maersk Alabama* when hijacked by Somalian pirates in 2009. Hero of the story and movie made about the incident. Bachelor's degree from Massachusetts Maritime Academy.
- **Lady Gaga.** American singer, songwriter, and actress. One of the best-selling musicians of all time. Dropped out of New York University after two years.
- **Bill Gates.** American entrepreneur and philanthropist. Founder and CEO of Microsoft. Dropped out of Harvard in his sophomore year.

The answer is neither current students nor alumni identify the professor among the first three choices. The British novelist and translator, Tim Parks, author of sixteen novels and nine nonfiction books, just does not make the cut.

## WHAT ARE OUR EXPECTATIONS FOR PROFESSORS?

So, what do we want from Tim Parks? Any way we look, he is the most qualified to behave in the role of professor:

- **Facts**. He underwent a rigorous and even daunting submersion in scholarly activities.
- **Beliefs**. He probably knows things that other mortals cannot see or conceive.
- **Feelings**. He deserves respect for his dedication to pursuing knowledge.
- **Opinions**. He must know things we don't.
- **Assumptions**. With all his writing, he must have lessons for us.
- **Bias**. Of course, a professor knows more than the rest of us.

## PROFESSORS "PROFESS"

You may ask, "How will Parks fulfill our expectations?" The answer may be, "he will profess," a term with two common meanings:

- To claim openly but often falsely that one has knowledge, a quality, or feeling.
- To affirm one's faith in or allegiance to a set of beliefs or code of conduct.

In both definitions, the person who professes is superior to those who listen. No interruption is needed in a formal authoritative presentation.

The classroom lecture is the most common form of professing. The professor has a single story to be told in detail. She is not looking for other explanations. She does not want to be challenged on her interpretations. She is the authority. Everyone else is a target of her expertise.

We do not find such steadfast devotion to being right in all professions. Lawyers learn to argue any side of an issue. Doctors are taught to pursue different diagnoses before ruling them out. Engineers prefer to experiment on better ways to fix things as opposed to knowing the only right way. The academy needs no such questioning.

## GREAT PROFESSORS

Because of the lecture method, we have many mediocre instructors in higher education. If a young person has one great teacher in high school and one great professor in college, he is lucky. If five great teachers in each place, he is blessed. Great teachers are all over the place but sometimes you must search them out.

How do you know when you have a great professor? Lots of ways. They inspire, motivate, provide unique insights, and encourage you to reflect, think, and understand.

Most of the time we identify great professors from a classroom experience. What process do we use? Why do people often disagree? Perhaps former U.S. Supreme Court Justice Potter Stewart can help us with the answer. In 1964, he famously said:

> I shall not today attempt further to define the kinds of material I understand to be embraced within that shorthand description ... "hard-core pornography" ... and perhaps I could never succeed in intelligibly doing so. But I know it when I see it.

We can draw wisdom from this statement. Sometimes good teaching does not fit well the tools we use to evaluate it. Sometimes we just apply common sense. We know it when we see it.

Maybe Descartes was right. "I think, therefore I am." Thus it is with great professors. They exist even though doctoral programs do not encourage their development. In most cases, they transcend the years of graduate study much as a cactus somehow blooms in a desert.

## PROFESSORIAL "INTELLIGENCE"

If we can't fully explain the essence of great professors, we can observe the difference between two qualities:

- **Book Intelligence**. A broad mental capability to reason, solve problems, and think abstractly. IQ tests measure potential educational achievement or predict job performance.
- **Emotional Intelligence**. The capacity to understand one's own emotions and those of others. Measured by success in interactions with others.

It is axiomatic to think that professors are intelligent, at least in the ways we measure logical and conceptual ability. The challenge is whether they are "smart." This is a different matter entirely. Do they apply book intelligence and motivate students to learn?

## Question
When it comes to helping others learn, is it more important to have a high book or emotional intelligence?

*Answer*
Emotional intelligence has an edge. It facilitates moving from feelings and opinions to facts and beliefs.

## Question
A professor with considerable book intelligence is asked, "What is the difference for students between work and play in the classroom?" What does he say?

*Answer*
Learning is not easy. It is hard work. It does not come easily. Play is what students do when they are not studying.

## Question
A professor with considerable emotional intelligence is asked the same question. What does she say?

*Answer*
Work is what we have to do. Play is what we want to do. Great professors help students play as they learn even though learning often requires effort.

## Question
A doctoral program prepares candidates for positions in the academy. Almost all the activity focuses on book intelligence. We asked professors, "Does this make any sense?" What did they say?

*Answer*
We did not get an answer. The individuals were too busy finishing up monographs for submission to a scholarly journal.

## GREAT PROFESSORS, CHICAGO CUBS

In 2016, the Chicago Cubs won the World Series for the first time in 108 years. Manager Joe Maddon got credit for the success. He offers a model for behavior in the classroom.

- He sets a framework and allows coaches and players to evolve on their own timeline. If someone is not performing, he works with them. He does relegate them to a position on the bench.
- He believes in and supports his players. He gives struggling hitters a chance to play and waits until they figure out why they are in a slump.
- He holds everyone accountable by introducing humor at tense moments. His team motto is "Try Not to Suck."
- He applies emotional intelligence. He knows when the team needs a break from the pressure and scrutiny and lightens the mood to reenergize the team.
- He gains respect before asking for performance.
- He explains why it is important to do a good job.

### Question
On the first day of class, a professor handed out a syllabus and told the class that she had high standards and expected students to meet them. Attend every class. Take notes. Read the textbook and be prepared to discuss it. Complete every assignment on time. How did things turn out?

*Answer*
Among other things she did not win an award as professor of the year. Cubs' manager Joe Maddon can explain why. What happened to the coaching?

### Question
A professor assigned teams of students to make a presentation to a panel of visiting business executives who would evaluate their goals, assumptions, and conclusions. The executives would assign a grade and the professor would announce a ranking of how all the teams did. The pressure grew intense. For the students, is this an example of working or playing?

*Answer*
Maybe playing for some teams. One group stayed in the computer lab through the night before the presentation. A member wrote on a smart

board, "2:15 am—we will kill the competition!" For most of the groups the presentations were off the chart. At a reception after the grades were announced, one student explained her group's feeling to an executive, "We worked like dogs on this project. We loved it."

## SECRET OF GREAT PROFESSORS

Putting aside the problem of poor performance in the classroom, what is the missing lesson in college teaching? It's simple, really. The secret of great professors is, "they engage students with 'sticky' stories."

A good story does several things. It is an account of people and events told for entertainment. It positions the professor as someone who has something useful and interesting to say. With real or imaginary people or events, a story causes the other party to remember you. If carefully chosen, it can motivate behavior.

In the classroom, the professor can expand sticky messages into engaging stories. The book *Made to Stick*, Chip and Dan Heath authors, (2007) offers six key attributes of a sticky message:

- **Stories.** Send a message in the form of a story.
- **Unexpectedness.** Start the story in one direction and end with a compelling outcome not foreseen in advance.
- **Concreteness.** The message should strike a responsive chord in others who had actual experiences related to it.
- **Credibility.** The idea should be believable and convincing.
- **Emotions.** The thought should be welcome and even pleasurable.
- **Simplicity.** The message should be easy to grasp.
- **Sharp.** The point should be compelling.

**Question**
We said "six key attributes" but listed seven. What happened?

*Answer*
We added "sharp" to spell out the acronym "**success.**"

**Question**
A blind man sitting on the ground in a plaza hopes to receive money from passersby. He posted a cardboard sign that simply said, "I'm blind. Please help." Is that a sticky message?

*Answer*
Not really. An Internet video illustrates the point. It shows a few individuals dropping money into a cup. A young woman changes the man's sign. Suddenly, many more people are giving the man money. She wrote, "It's a beautiful day and I can't see it."

## CONTRADICTION FOR PROFESSORS

Faculty members are surrounded by efforts of their institutions to disseminate sticky messages when recruiting students. We see things like the following:

- "Only $12,000 a year tuition."
- "90 percent of graduates have jobs in three months."
- "Average salary is $43,000."
- "Small classes."
- "Professors who care."
- "Successful graduates who succeed."

**Question**
Do these messages stick in the minds of students and parents?

*Answer*
Maybe once upon a time. As just about every college uses the same exact messages, nothing sticks.

**Question**
The basketball team of a little-known college had an exceptional year and was invited to participate in the NCAA "March madness" where it won four games and was on national television twice. What happened?

*Answer*
A sticky message. Applications rose 120 percent the next year.

**Question**
Nick Saban became the coach of The University of Alabama football team in 2007. The team won the national champion in 2009, 2011, 2012, and 2015. The University pays Nick $7,000,000 a year. Is he worth it?

*Answer*
See the answer to the previous question. "Alabama, national champion!" Sticky message.

## STICKY DOES NOT STAND ALONE

Advertisers understand the importance of sticky messages. "A diamond is forever." "Good to the last drop." "The Breakfast of Champions." The message may be a lie. A bride may lose her diamond ring. Folgers coffee is undrinkable after sitting in the pot for six hours. Weaklings eat Wheaties.

Another way to illustrate the role of sticky messages in communications is to use famous lines from movies. Once again, show the class something like famous quotes and ask them to identify the actor, movie, or year.

> Frankly, my dear, I don't give a damn
> Clark Gable, *Gone with the Wind*, 1939
> I'm going to make him an offer he can't refuse
> Marlon Brando, *The Godfather*, 1972
> All right, Mr. DeMille, I'm ready for my close-up
> Gloria Swanson, *Sunset Boulevard*, 1950
> May the Force be with you
> Harrison Ford, *Star Wars*, 1977
> Round up the usual suspects
> Claude Rains, *Casablanca*, 1942
> I'll get you, my pretty, and your little dog too!
> Margaret Hamilton, *The Wizard of Oz*, 1939
> I'm king of the world!
> Leonardo DiCaprio, *Titanic*, 1997

## CONTEXT OF THE STORIES

The sticky message only works in higher education when accompanied by a powerful context, the setting or circumstances where it is delivered. In a classroom, a successful teacher interacts easily with students. In a distance-learning environment, she adjusts the teaching style.

**Question**
A professor was directing an Internet discussion session in a distance-learning course. The students logged in and all communications were posted on a website. She asked students to rank, in terms of the level of corruption, China; Poland; India; Brazil; Saudi Arabia; Botswana; Italy; and Argentina. Which country ranked the highest? The lowest?

*Answer*
Argentina ranked highest. Students knew about the beauty of Buenos Aires, the Pampas, and Andes mountains. Botswana was identified as the most

corrupt. Students assumed a country in Africa has a high level of corruption. This shows two forms of context:

- **Learning Context.** Students had impressions. Both guesses are dead wrong. Botswana was the least and Argentina was most corrupt.
- **Classroom Context.** Because students committed themselves in advance, they were highly interested in the results.

She finished with a discussion of impressions and told stories of mistakes we make when we jump to conclusions. A follow-up survey of students showed they enjoyed the mixture of stories and context.

## CONTEXT OF "PRISON"

Malcolm Gladwell relates a compelling story about how students are affected by context. A professor at Stanford University created a "prison" with four small cells painted black with steel-barred doors. He randomly divided volunteers into "guards" with uniforms and dark glasses and "prisoners" also with uniforms.

Real police arrested the "prisoner" volunteers at their homes at night. They were cuffed, brought to a police station, fingerprinted, blindfolded, brought to the cells, and stripped. The number on each uniform was their only identification.

The "guards" created an atmosphere of terror. The prisoners experienced emotional depression, anxiety, and rage. The fourteen-day experiment had to be cancelled after six days. The exercise showed how context overwhelms normal behavior. Even guards, who had identified themselves as pacifists, participated in the terrorizing actions.

## GREAT TEACHERS DISPEL MISCONCEPTIONS

One of the highest forms of learning occurs when our beliefs and assumptions are challenged. This lesson comes across most effectively when students stake out a position and then confront evidence that contradicts it.

### Question
A professor explained that groups of people working together often produce more accurate results than a single researcher. He asked students what they thought was the level of accuracy of Wikipedia and the Encyclopedia Britannica. Students were quite sure that the encyclopedia took great pains

to ensure accuracy while Wikipedia did not. Does evidence confirm the student view?

*Answer*
Not at all. *Nature* magazine compared Wikipedia and Britannica's. Errors were found in both but they were quite close. Wikipedia had four and the encyclopedia three errors per article. A Nottingham University study using graduate students had a similar result.

## CAN LEARNING BE FUN?

Humor can be a powerful feature of learning. A professor can use it to engage students so they stop watching the clock. When class ends as a surprise, we have the best chance to create learning.

### Question
The goal of a class session is to encourage students to focus on the content of a message instead of its delivery. Not what the person said or wrote in a text or e-mail. Rather, what did the person mean?

A professor starts by saying, "It is important to say things clearly. As an example, no one can figure out the meaning of the following quote."

> *Accodrnig to Cmabrigde Uinervtisy rscheearch, the oredr of ltteers in a wrod deos not mttaer, the olny iprmoetnt tihng is taht the frist and lsat ltteer be in the rghit pclae.*
>
> *The rset can be a total mses and you can sitll raed it wouthit a porbelm. Tihs is bcuseae the huamn mnid deos not raed ervey lteter by istlef, but the wrod as a wlohe.*

What will be the reaction of the students?

*Answer*
Obviously, they can read it. They will protest the statement that they can't. An instructor can play with them as they prove their point. The interaction sets up a realization that words can have a hidden meaning. They should not jump to conclusions but rather should look for the real message.

### Question
A little girl brought to school a picture of mommy at work. The little girl wants to do the same job. Look at the picture. What does the mother do?

*Answer*
She works at Home Depot. Figure 6.1 shows her selling snow shovels.

Figure 6.1    Little Girl's Mom at Work. *Source*: Tracey Tango

## WHO IS TO BLAME?

We have a lesson here. The failure of many professors to deliver sticky messages in the right context and perhaps with humor is at the center of the problem in higher education today. We ignore the evidence at our own peril. More than half of four-year college courses are now taught by part-timers. Tenured faculty members change jobs at considerable risk because no one wants to hire and tenure them. Outstanding teachers are denied long-term appointments.

How serious is the problem that we are conditioned to think a PhD along with a dissertation is the primary qualification for a professor? Pretty serious. Who should we blame? Let's take a look.

## BEAUMONT UNIVERSITY "STORY"

What do parents and students want in the professors teaching in colleges and universities? We tested this question with graduate students, mostly employed, some already with college-age children. A classroom exercise starts with an ad in the *Chronicle of Higher Education*.

> Beaumont University seeks an assistant professor of management to teach BS and MBA courses. Preference will be given to individuals who have appropriate

academic credentials, teaching experience, and scholarly writing. Submit a CV and cover letter as instructed in the job description.

Next, we give students a summary of the qualifications of eight candidates. Seven have PhDs. One has two master's degrees.

Working in groups, students select three people to interview ranked in order of preference. After they reveal their choices, we learn they picked "the most qualified candidates." At the same time, the groups never agree on the top choices. They argue on the merits of degrees, scholarship, experiences, and other details.

**Question**
The interactive discussion ends with a question, "What are we looking for in a professor?" What do students say?

*Answer*
The responses are always the same. Degrees, scholarship, and teaching experience.

**Question**
Then we ask, "Who will be the best person to encourage learning? Which candidate wants to encourage students to learn? Which one do you think the students would like to have as a teacher?" What do they say now?

*Answer*
The result is silence followed by an acknowledgment that they don't know. No group gave much thought to those questions.

Soon, we are having a different discussion. Students assumed that an advanced degree qualifies someone to be a professor without much consideration of what professors do. They ignored whether the person wanted to teach, publish, or do something else. They needed no information on whether a person would fit into an academic or any other setting.

This is the same situation when a search committee designs an ad, accepts and screens replies, and chooses candidates to interview. Even if the application has glowing information on teaching desire and success, it is largely ignored in the absence of a doctorate that required a dissertation.

## CHANGE OF PERSPECTIVE

The Beaumont story is not over. Prior to using the exercise in several classes, we had a discussion on three factors that come right out of Human Resources 101:

- Qualifications—Can the person do the job?
- Attitude—Does the person want to do the job?
- Personal chemistry—Do we like the person?

When we subsequently did the exercise, the student reaction was radically different. Most teams wanted to interview the only candidate who did not have a doctorate. His two master's degrees were accepted along with information that he had excellent student evaluations. The convincing point was a quote he included:

> Average teachers inspire students to get high grades. Great teachers inspire them to fulfill their destiny.

This is a sticky message. The quote made all the difference but only after students were alerted to the deeply ingrained assumption that a PhD solves all.

## OPENING A DOOR TO REFORM

The Beaumont University exercise gives us a snapshot of public perception about the academy. It is not just a problem of the professoriate. As a society, we generally agree that the doctorate is the most important factor in selecting professors for the classroom.

> Ninety-two percent of our professors have Ph.Ds.
> Dr. Jones has a Ph.D from Harvard.

These are the proud messages of the admissions office when recruiting. They appeal to parents and students alike.

The graduate students who preferred credentials to evidence of effective teaching were somewhat chagrined in the later discussions. They acknowledged their own academic experience was a mixed blessing. Great professors alongside mediocre instructors, even though both groups had prestigious degrees awarded, schools attended, and publications written.

Not a single graduate student ever said doctoral-level professors were better than masters-level instructors. This is a rather interesting finding for any discussion of reforms to the academy.

## CONCLUSION

It may be understandable that professors are not the first choice of students in front of the classroom. It is not easy to compete with Captain Richard Phillips or Lady Gaga. If they are the last choice, or no choice at all, that is not good.

A lecture without a compelling story goes nowhere. A classroom lacking interactive communications virtually shuts down after a few minutes. Sticky messages, compelling stories, the right context, and engagement humor are critical elements of effective teaching and indeed lead to greatness for some instructors.

*Chapter Seven*

# Professor, Can You Ever Be Wrong? Do You Understand What Happens If You Don't Agree with Me?

> Those who think they know it all are very annoying to those of us who do.
> —Robert K. Muller, author and executive

### BELIEVE IT OR NOT

An undergraduate took a political science class and completed a four-question mid-term essay exam. He received a grade of "C." It took a month to schedule an appointment with the professor.

*Student:* "I do not understand why I got a C."

*Professor:* "Let me look. Hmm, you got 25 points on the first question, 23 on the second, 21 on the third, and 24 on the last." A pause. "Tell you what. If you get a B on the final, I'll give you a B for the course."

*Student:* "But I got a 93 on the mid-term" (90 to 100 was an A). "Can you just give me an A on the mid-term?"

*Professor:* "I told you. Get a B on the final and you get a B for the course."

The outcome? The student left, did not study for the final, got a B for the course, and never took another course with the professor. A few years later the professor resigned and left to become president of another university.

## ALPHA MALES AND FEMALES

In social animals, the alpha male or female is the individual with the highest rank. Alphas gain preferential access to food and desirable activities. Alphas achieve their status by superior physical prowess or building alliances within the group.

The academy knows the behavior well. The alpha category is achieved by completing a doctoral program with a dissertation and publishing in scholarly journals.

## ILLUSIONARY SUPERIORITY

Another view of professors is explained in something called the Dunning–Kruger effect where low-ability individuals have a superiority complex. Surviving a dissertation effort might cause this to happen. It works two ways:

- **Inept Professors.** Professors who are largely incompetent do not recognize their inability to teach or help students learn. They accuse others of failing to perform to their high standards.
- **"Genius" Professors.** They understand complex and obscure concepts and may erroneously assume that such insights are easy for their students.

### Question
In 1981, Robert Shiller, a Yale professor, demonstrated that stock markets are irrational. He won the Nobel Prize in Economics in 2013. Robert Merton, an MIT professor, disagreed, saying markets are efficient and investors could not take advantage of inefficiencies. He won the Nobel Prize in 1997. Who was right?

*Answer*
Shiller was right. In 1994, Merton became a founder of Long-Term Capital Management (LTCM), a hedge fund designed to take advantage of market inefficiencies. It used complex statistics and high leverage. It earned 40 percent a year until 1997. The Russian and Asian financial crises in 1998 caused it to lose $5 billion. It closed in 2000.

> As of this writing, Merton did not return his Nobel Prize.

## PROFESSOR HUMOR

Professors tend to be experts in all areas. This encourages poking fun at them.

1. One day a college professor, after getting irritated in a college classroom, stood up in front of the class and said, "If anyone is an idiot, he or she should stand up now." After a minute a young man stood up.

*Professor:* Do you actually believe that you are an idiot?

*Student:* Well, no, I just don't want to see you standing there all by yourself.

2. A professor and his spouse went on a camping trip. After enjoying dinner and a bottle of wine, they retired for the night. A few hours later, the spouse nudged the professor:

*Spouse:* Honey, look up at the sky and tell me what you see.

*Professor:* I see millions and millions of stars.

*Spouse:* And what do you deduce from that?

*Professor:* Astronomically, it tells me that there are millions of galaxies and potentially billions of planets.

*Spouse:* What else?

*Professor:* Astrologically, I can observe that Saturn is in Leo. Horologically, I deduce that the time is approximately a quarter past three. Meteorologically, I suspect that we will have a beautiful day tomorrow. Theologically, I can see that God is all powerful, and that we are a small and insignificant part of the universe.

*Spouse:* Is that all?

*Professor:* What does it tell you?

*Spouse:* Well, I am curious to find out who stole our tent.

## KNOWLEDGE AND EXPERTISE

Professors often think they are experts when they are not. They are confident when no evidence or logic supports their beliefs. Why does this happen? One reason is scholarly research can fail to distinguish between science and art. Science reveals nature and basic principles. Art is an applied skill.

A major problem of pursuing a doctoral degree is we subconsciously behave as though we are scientists. We become experts in a narrow slice of knowledge and expand feelings of superiority into other areas.

Serious scholarship does not change art into science. We cannot replicate the findings from most dissertations. Even the most precise scholarly research is shaped by beliefs, interpretations, and limitations. The most widely read and astute professor can get it wrong.

This problem does not affect every discipline equally. In the physical sciences, engineering, and medicine, we can verify many ideas and replicate them. This is much more difficult to do in the social sciences, education, and business. What worked yesterday may not work today. Thus, we often get it wrong in new situations.

**Question**

An expert made the statement, "Half of the people of a country will be wealthier than the average." Is this statement true?

*Answer*

Not necessarily. Nassim Taleb gives an example where 70 percent have a salary higher than the average.

| | |
|---|---|
| Total population | 100 |
| Net income of seventy people | $50,000 |
| Net income of thirty people | $10,000 |
| Average salary | $38,500 (70% × 50,000 + 30% × 10,000) |

**Question**

A company hires one hundred managers and puts them in a young-leaders training program. Sixty percent succeed and 40 percent fail. When they succeed, they are promoted. We repeat the process several times and arrive at the following.

| Start | Promoted | Dropped Out |
|---|---|---|
| 100 | 60 | 40 |
| 60 | 36 | 24 |
| 36 | 21 | 15 |
| 21 | 12 | 9 |
| 12 | 7 | 5 |
| 7 | 4 | 3 |

We finish with four individuals. Does this prove they are competent and efficient?

*Answer*

Not necessarily. We could have a population made up entirely of bad managers. Some will succeed. Randomness allows some people to succeed and others to fail.

## SILENT EVIDENCE

A serious weakness of our level of confidence occurs because of silent evidence.

- **Unknown Silent Evidence.** A college president told his friends that he got the job because the search committee found him to be fully qualified. Did he tell them he had a friend on the committee who spread lies about other candidates?
- **Known Silent Evidence.** A professor received negative evaluations from several students. Should she be denied tenure? Suppose the comments arose from a disgruntled student who incited fellow students to turn in bad evaluations?

### Question
A journal asks two experts to review all scholarly submissions anonymously. Does this guarantee high quality?

*Answer*
Maybe yes and maybe no. Many of us share our research at conferences and in working papers that are widely circulated among our peers. By the time a work is submitted for formal publication, everyone knows who wrote it. It may be accepted or rejected for many reasons as an exception to the announced "anonymous" review process.

### Question
An editor asked two professors to read a submission and make a recommendation. The first said it was a major contribution to the literature. The second said it was faulty and even embarrassing. What should the editor do?

*Answer*
Whatever the answer, we should recognize that academic research often has biases and disagreement.

## MISTAKE OF KNOWING

We should respect the insights and knowledge that emerges for professorial scholarship. At the same time, overconfidence is dangerous. Political scientists, historians, economists, and others create knowledge from data or observation under a specific set of circumstances. A problem arises when they defend their efforts. The harder they are pushed, the more confident they become.

**Question**
What is an example of the mistake of knowing?

*Answer*
Political forecasting from a database. A professor gathers past presidential voting data, builds a model, and applies it to current conditions. Because things change, the relationships may no longer work. This is often not acknowledged.

**Question**
How about another example?

*Answer*
An economist builds a model to forecast gross domestic product. He takes all the data from 2010 to 2014 and converts it into a hundred formulas showing relationships. Things change. In 2017, the model fails to predict the performance of the economy.

**Question**
What happens if the political scientist and economist were seriously wrong in the predictions from their models?

*Answer*
Nothing if they have tenure. They just return to their universities and wait for another chance.

## CAUSATION AND CORRELATION

Our level of confidence in academic scholarship is affected by two concepts.

- **Causation**. A relationship where one event increases the probability of the occurrence of a second event.
- **Correlation**. An indicator of the strength and direction of a relationship between two variables.

**Question**
Researchers tested the speed of work under different light conditions. Workers in a factory assembled components as overhead lights were

diminished in brightness. A control group had full light for the entire experiment. Both groups steadily increased production. What is the relationship between the level of light and the speed of productivity?

*Answer*
We cannot tell from this experiment between 1924 and 1927. Called the "Hawthorne effect," both groups responded to the attention they received as opposed to the degree of light. This is an important lesson. Get causation right before we confidently explain phenomena.

## CAN A PROFESSOR PREDICT AN ELECTION RESULT?

Psephology deals with the scientific analysis of elections. It uses historical data, public opinion surveys, campaign spending by candidates, and other data to predict voting outcomes.

Many professors apply their research skills to forecast the results of elections. This applies to economists, historians, social scientists, statisticians, and others. Who got it right and wrong in 2016? These were the results of the prominent academic forecasters.

- **Allan Lichtman.** This professor of history at American University predicted a Trump victory six weeks before the election. He used the answers to thirteen true/false questions dealing with 2014 congressional elections, level of economic activity, candidate charisma, and other factors.
- **Ray Fair.** This Yale University economics professor used macroeconomic modeling to predict a Trump win with Clinton getting 44 percent of the total vote. She got 51 percent.
- **Alan Abramowitz.** This Emory College political science professor predicted Trump would win the popular vote when he did not. He based the prediction on Barack Obama's incumbency and approval rating and the growth in gross national product.
- **Arie Kapteyn.** This University of Southern California professor was criticized by the *New York Times* for repeatedly interviewing the same individuals. He showed Trump winning by 3 percent of the popular vote.
- **Jacob Montgomery and Florian Hollenbach.** These Washington University and Texas A&M professors had data showing a Republican should win except for the fact that Trump was too different. Because of this "Trump tax," the model was right but the prediction was wrong.
- **Helmut Norpoth.** This Stony Brook University professor said, "It is 87 to 99 percent certain that Donald Trump will win the presidential election." He made the prediction nine months earlier based on results in the

primaries and the fact that electoral pendulum swings back to the party out of office after an incumbent has served two terms.

Two forecasters deserve a little more attention.

## Sam Wang

This professor of molecular biology and neuroscience at Princeton University could not be further away from politics as his work focuses on the neurobiology of learning. From this background, he forecasts election results.

- In 2004, Wang predicted the actual electoral college outcome.
- In 2012, he correctly predicted the presidential vote outcome in forty-nine of fifty states.
- In 2016, professor Wang initially predicted a 93 percent chance for a Hillary Clinton win. He then raised the probability to 99 percent.

## Nate Silver

This American statistician analyzes politics and sports and predicts outcomes. In 2008, his successful forecasts brought national and international recognition. In 2016, Silver protested that the country was deeply unsettled and a win by Donald Trump was a definite possibility. So was a Clinton landslide. The outcome was simply too unpredictable to forecast.

**Question**
Is there any chance Mr. Silver will join a college or university on a tenure-track appointment and carry on his work from the academy?

*Answer*
Not likely. A search committee will probably notice that his only academic credential is a bachelor of arts degree in economics from the University of Chicago.

**Question**
Two candidates ran for public office. Candidate X spent $2 million. Y spent $400,000. X won with 56 percent of the vote. What is the relationship between campaign spending and votes obtained?

*Answer*
The economist Steven Levitt found campaign spending barely affects the number of votes. He argued that candidate attractiveness, not spending, is the causal factor for finding winners.

**Question**
In the 2016 U.S. presidential campaign, Donald Trump raised $800 million. Hillary Clinton raised $1.3 billion. If we ask a group of six professors whether these results of the election validate Levitt's findings, what would they say?

*Answer*
Some would cite the evidence as being compelling. Others would disagree. The conversation would be peppered with contradictory theories built upon prior research. Maybe we passed the trait on to our students who voted in 2016 largely based on trivial and misrepresented social media presentations.

**Question**
Ms. Clinton received three million more total votes than Mr. Trump. Right after the election, Mr. Trump claimed he won more votes from voters legally authorized to vote. What does this show?

*Answer*
After you are wrong, you can argue you were right. Your friends will agree with you. Your enemies will not.

## UNDUE CONFIDENCE

One of the dangers of excessive confidence is a failure to accept that one's work has flaws. Criticism about a weakness in a dissertation, statement in a classroom, or presentation of research findings can produce anxiety or anger. These feelings encourage resistance to changing a viewpoint when new evidence is introduced and can lead to bad behavior, whether in the classroom or faculty meetings.

## CATS AND CONFIDENCE

Five teams of students were given ten minutes to estimate the number of cats and dogs in U.S. homes and to indicate their levels of confidence in the estimates. How did they do?

*Answer*
The estimates of cats in millions were 200, 14, 12, 8, and 2. Four teams were highly confident. One team stated it had no clue. The actual answer was ninety-three million.

**Question**
After being told the number of cats, the groups were asked to share their estimates for dogs. They asked for permission to change the estimates. Given such permission, what was the range for dogs?

*Answer*
The estimate of dogs ranged from fifty-five to eighty million. The actual number was sixty-five million.

**Question**
The students then estimated reptiles, primates, and big cats in U.S. homes. What do you think happened?

*Answer*
They were all over the place, but there was one big difference. The groups were much less confident. The actual numbers were two million reptiles, fifteen thousand primates, and fifteen thousand big cats.

**Lesson Learned:** Perhaps professors can learn something from cats and their students. It may be commonplace to be confident when we lack information or are just outright wrong. Defending erroneous findings or data is not praiseworthy.

## BOZO EXPLOSION IN THE ACADEMY

A combination of the trials of the dissertation, illusions of superiority, and undue confidence come together in a concept popularized by Steve Jobs when he was CEO of Apple. He observed skilled and competent people ranging from "A," the most talented, through "B" and "C" down to "D" for someone who is totally inept. In the hiring process:

- "A" players hire "A" players so they get people as good as themselves. Even better, they are not afraid to hire "A+" players.
- "B" players hire "C" players and "C" players hire "D" players. In both cases the goal is to feel superior to others. Not to mention that they do not want to be hiring their replacements.

The slang term "bozo" referring to an idiot has come to mean a "B" player in charge of hiring. Such a person becomes a "bozo bomber" when hiring practices over time steadily decrease the competence level of an organization.

**Question**
Could a bozo explosion happen in the academy?

*Answer*
It already did. Many years ago, professors decided that the best candidates for presidents and deans were the most successful scholars. When faced with management and administrative tasks, they were not skilled in selecting "A" players. Today the academy has a surplus of bozos in administration.

**Question**
Could a bozo explosion occur in the ranks of the faculty?

*Answer*
It, too, has occurred. Professors participating on search committees do not want to be surrounded by more productive scholars, better teachers, or even strong colleagues. They often vote for hiring and tenure for marginal teachers and scholars.

**Question**
Members of a search committee often know they are making a bad decision on a soon-to-be colleague. Why is it so hard to back up and realize what is happening?

*Answer*
If you cannot answer this question, please go back and read the chapter again.

## CONCLUSION

We have considerable evidence that professors enter the academy with more confidence than justified by their overall package of knowledge and skills. This partly explains the resistance to reform the dissertation process, activities leading to tenure, teaching formats, and other features of the academy that need to change.

*Chapter Eight*

# Why Do Students Fail to Learn What I Fail to Teach? Why Did Nobody Tell Me Nothing about Teaching?

In a completely rational society, the best of us would be teachers and the rest of us would have to settle for something less.

—Lee Iacocca, automobile company executive

### BELIEVE IT OR NOT

A rather amazing professor taught a course on the history of Russia and China. He interacted smoothly with students in a lecture format but never seemed to know anyone's name. The situation needed to be corrected.

*Professor:* What can I do for you today?

*Student:* I just want to tell you that I did really well on your exam.

*Professor:* Why are you telling me that?

*Student:* Because I want you to remember me and my name when you read my paper.

*Professor:* OK. I can do that.

The outcome was a grade A in the course. Fifteen months later the professor was a member of a faculty committee that awarded the student honors upon graduation.

# Chapter Eight

# STYLE, SITUATIONS, AND PRACTICES IN TEACHING

An instructor usually arrives with specific ideas about teaching. Most of these will not work well.

**Question**
What teaching style is most common?

*Answer*
Stand in front of the class and talk in the general direction of people sitting in student chairs or at tables. Boring.

**Question**
Will the inexperienced professor have to make a situational adjustment in the class?

*Answer*
Of course. If it took five to seven years to get a degree, the new teacher will be totally unprepared for the average undergraduate classroom. Technology has changed how high schools prepare students to learn.

**Question**
A new professor came to the first day of class. He faced sixteen students even though his roster showed twenty-four registered. He instructed the class to read chapters one and two in the textbook. How did it go for the second class?

*Answer*
Fifteen students arrived on time. Seven students came late. Two students were not registered for the course. Eight students "looked at" chapter 1. Eleven students had not yet bought the textbook.

**Question**
What did the professor do about the situation on day two?

*Answer*
He realized he had a lot to learn about being a teacher.

**Question**
A direct style of teaching exists when a professor tells the students what to do, how to do it, and when it needs to be done. Information is delivered via lectures supported by assigned readings and audiovisual presentations. Students learn course material by listening, taking notes, and studying for exams. How does this work for the new instructor?

*Answer*
In many cases, students hate it.

**Question**
With a discussion style, the instructor encourages critical thinking and lively interaction with students. She asks students to respond to challenging questions and is a facilitator guiding students to learning. How does this work for the new instructor?

*Answer*
Good, even though new instructors tend not to use it. The direct style is most common.

**Question**
With a delegation style, the instructor assigns tasks that students work on independently, either individually or in groups. Students learn from each other and from feedback provided by the instructor when tasks are finished. How does this work for the new instructor?

*Answer*
We don't know. It rarely is done.

**Question**
With an innovation style, the new instructor does something different and memorable to promote learning. How does this work for the new instructor?

*Answer*
Although extremely rare, it can work well if an instructor has the skills to do it.

## SPEAKING UP INNOVATION

A social sciences class was examining the "halo effect," a bias in people so they see someone more positively than a situation might justify. We know physically attractive individuals are assumed to possess more socially desirable traits, live happier lives, and become more successful than unattractive people. We do not always realize that people who speak up produce the same positive reaction.

This was tested in a classroom experiment on the importance of being noticed. After several interactive sessions, students were given a case study alleging medical malpractice against a hospital. A lawsuit had been filed. The students were directed to bring to class a one-page summary of the issues. When they arrived, they were divided into two groups:

- **Group 1**. Eight students were told they would participate in an executive committee meeting chaired by the instructor. The goal was to discuss whether to settle the lawsuit.
- **Group 2**. Eighteen students were to observe the meeting.

Each candidate in Group 1 was assigned a role not known to other class members. The roles were as follows:

- Block the effort to reach a consensus.
- Try to get the group to agree to a low offer to settle.
- Try to get the group to agree to a high offer to settle.
- Try to distract the group from the topic at hand.
- Serve as the chief financial officer.
- Serve as hospital general counsel.

Two students were assigned to simply speak more words than any other participant. Both were selected because they hardly ever said anything previously in class and they were largely invisible to the other students.

The candidates in Group 2 were told that each person had been given an assigned behavior. They were to observe the meeting and identify the assignment given to each student. The meeting lasted for twenty minutes. Then it was stopped.

The observers ranked the participants from most to least contributions. Next they ranked the participants on who spoke the most words. The rankings were identical. The best performer spoke the most words.

## Question
Now the observers were ready to identify the roles. One of the two students assigned the role of speaking the most words failed to accept the challenge. Speaking the fewest words, the student was rated as the weakest performer. The observers did not even have a guess as to the assigned role. As they moved up the ranking, the observers got some roles right but entirely missed others.

Finally, the group got to the top performer who spoke the most words. How did they do?

*Answer*
The class came to life with confidence that they knew the assigned behavior. They acknowledged the individual had been quiet and largely unknown

for most of the course term. Still, they were virtually unanimous that the individual was directed *to display leadership qualities*!

**Learning Took Place.** When the observers were told that the assigned goal simply involved words spoken, many lessons were immediately identified. One was the importance of talking in support of others. It made the speaker likable. Another was engagement improves the quality of our performance.

## FEEDBACK

Instruction improves when professors seek feedback on what they are doing. Unfortunately, it is often dismissed. "Students are lazy. They do not want to work. Admissions standards are slipping."

### Question
Several guides to effective teaching encourage the use of all four styles. The direct style is recommended early in the course and the other styles are introduced later. Does this work?

*Answer*
Maybe but why wait to introduce the good stuff? Lecture for ten minutes, discuss, delegate, and innovate in each class right from the start.

## WHAT DO NEW INSTRUCTORS NEED TO KNOW?

Teaching involves mechanics and structure. Professors need a little coaching before they enter a classroom.

### Question
Teaching always should involve some presentation. What coaching is needed here?

*Answer*
Use a style that is comfortable for you but also that works. Talk to other instructors and see how they do it.

### Question
A syllabus is an outline of subjects in a course. It sets up student expectations and guides them through the course. What coaching is needed here?

*Answer*
Pay a lot of attention to creating a syllabus. Don't overload it with detail or too many requirements. Put in important stuff but less is more.

### Question
Even though the course has a title and textbook, the instructors get to make real choices on content to be covered. What coaching is needed here?

*Answer*
Set up the curriculum in a way that you can deliver it. Line it up with your standards and expectations but be realistic on goals and expectations. Whatever else, be organized with coordinated class sessions, materials, and assignments.

### Question
An academic standard is a level of quality or attainment in a course or degree program. What coaching is needed here?

*Answer*
Learn department standards on coverage of material, attendance, missed exams, and plagiarism. Align the course with them.

### Question
Everybody knows a grade is a letter, number, or both, indicating the relative quality of a student's work in a course, examination, or special assignment. What coaching is needed here?

*Answer*
Be fair and reasonable in terms of student expectations but be careful not to be at odds with university guidelines and department norms.

### Question
Learning outcomes describe what students can expect to know after taking and passing a program or course. What coaching is needed here?

*Answer*
A school or department may provide guidelines for learning outcomes. The new instructor will probably forget them because they are nebulous at the level of the classroom.

### Question
If learning outcomes can be ignored, why do we have them?

*Answer*
Accrediting bodies, professional educators, and politicians want to measure improvement in learning. The most widely used yardsticks are exams that reflect short-term knowledge. Except for student evaluations, most schools have no idea whether you achieve their stated learning outcomes. Just be a good and caring teacher and everything else takes care of itself.

## Question
An instructor is seeking a classic model for her course syllabus. A mentor advised her to think of the U.S. Constitution rather than the Declaration of Independence. Is this the right way to go?

*Answer*
Yes. The Constitution was written as a specific and legalistic set of guidelines. The Declaration of Independence is lofty and idealistic. In life, we encourage our students to pursue visions. In class, we want them to achieve specific knowledge and understanding.

## Question
At the start of most courses, undergraduate students do not have enough experience to make important contributions to classroom discussions. We should not expect too much. Do you agree?

*Answer*
Not at all and it is dangerous to make that assumption. If you project low expectations onto students, you are likely to be underestimating them.

## Question
You have been assigned to a course with a mandatory textbook. It contains too much material to cover in the course. What should you do?

*Answer*
Cover a portion of the textbook and add to it based on your own knowledge and beliefs. You have leeway to provide more emphasis in areas of your interest or expertise.

## Question
A university recommends awarding the grade of A to no more than 20 percent of students and Bs to no more than 40 percent. Should a new instructor follow these guidelines?

*Answer*
Bad policy. No right answer here. Rigidity in grading undermines learning. Some examples follow.

## Question
A student is scheduled to take a final exam. The student requests a makeup exam because her employer has forced her to work overtime restricting her ability to study. Should the instructor approve the request?

*Answer*
Whatever your answer, not everyone will agree with it.

**Question**
A student turned in a paper and received a grade of C. The student appealed requesting a chance to redo the paper. On the second submission, the instructor assigned a grade of B minus. The student appealed again explaining his employer reimbursed tuition for grades of B plus and above. The grade of B minus will cost him $2,700. Would you give the student another chance to improve the grade?

*Answer*
Whatever your answer, not everyone will agree with it.

**Question**
One of your students worked hard on a project but does not have the skills to get it right. The grade for effort would be an A but the grade for writing and content would be an F. What would you do?

*Answer*
Whatever your answer, not everyone will agree with it.

**Question**
A professor assigned students to a research project on the political climate of a country of their choosing. One student selected Italy and turned in a paper that deserved the grade of B. The instructor learned that the student had turned in a paper in another course on the economics of Italy. It was likely that much of the research for the political paper had been done for the previous class. What would you do about the grade?

*Answer*
Whatever your answer, not everyone will agree with it.

**Question**
An instructor is firm on the importance of proper English in the writing of research papers. A student turned in a paper that deserved an A for content and a C for writing. The instructor rejected the paper and the student appealed. Do you agree with the action?

*Answer*
Whatever your answer, not everyone will agree with it.

## ENCOUNTER OVER A SYLLABUS

A newly hired department chair arrived on campus and found himself in a discussion with the former department head:

*Former Chair:* I need to warn you about Ms. Garcia. She is an adjunct instructor that I banned from teaching any more courses.

*New Chair:* Why is that?

*Former Chair:* The students hate her. She received poor student evaluations.

*New Chair:* Thanks for the tip.

Subsequently, the new chair received conflicting reports. Faculty members said good things about Ms. Garcia and many students confirmed their reports. He scheduled a meeting with her.

*New Chair:* Why do you think you receive such poor student evaluations?

*Ms. Garcia:* I have no idea. It makes no sense.

*New Chair:* Do you explain your course at the start? Tell students what you expect? Give them information on the textbook? Assignments? Grading?

*Ms. Garcia:* Yes, of course. I explain clearly my expectations. Six bi-weekly quizzes, a midterm and final exam, a term paper, and one class presentation. Plus, excessive absences reduce grades.

**Question**
After this discussion, what happened?

*Answer*
The chair explained the danger of too many assignments without time for depth and reflection. She agreed to make changes. The chair reinstated her for a single course that was well received. Two years later she was offered a full-time appointment in the department.

## CONCLUSION

Every instructor develops a teaching style that combines knowledge, skills, and personal values. To be successful, the instructor must learn the requirements of the school, views of colleagues, and the expectations of students. The actual behaviors of instructors in classes span a wide range and students select, when they have the option, instructors that meet their personal preferences.

*Chapter Nine*

# What Is Your Problem with Students Sleeping in Class? Would It Bother You if a Student Asked You to Keep It Down?

> Some people talk in their sleep. Lecturers talk while other people sleep.
>
> —Albert Camus, philosopher

### BELIEVE IT OR NOT

An instructor was truly horrible in the classroom. Boring, boring, boring. The opinion was unanimous. Students complained incessantly. The dean met with the department chair.

*Dean:* We have a real problem with Edmundson.

*Department Chair:* Tell me about it.

*Dean:* Why did you change him from a one-hour class three days a week to a three-hour class that meets only Tuesday mornings?

*Department Chair:* If he meets once a week, I get fewer complaints.

*Dean:* Do you know he keeps students in class for only about an hour?

*Department Chair:* Yes.

*Dean:* He is not teaching the full class period. What are you going to do about it?

*Department Chair:* Nothing. If I have a horrible teacher everybody is happy when the class finishes real early.

*Dean:* No response.

We know the goals of the lecture. Now we might remove a few drawbacks. Let's look at techniques that enhance the classroom.

## PROBLEMS WITH THE COURSE

Every professor can do better in a classroom when he or she develops a strategy to deal with a problem. Examples.

- **Poor Lecturer**. You simply are not good at preparing and delivering lectures. Your voice is monotone, you have an innate shyness, or you are uncomfortable answering questions without reflecting upon them.
- **Weak Preparation**. You are assigned to teach a course where you are not comfortable with the subject matter.
- **Bad Textbook**. It is selected by the department and is confusing or too difficult for the students.

The opposite side of this coin occurs when problems arise from the students. An example is a large class that you cannot control. Students may pay no attention, refuse to engage in questions and answers, or are rude or unruly.

### Question
A student was completing the course evaluation at the end of a semester. The last entry was, "In the space below write any overall comment on this course or the instructor not covered above." The student wrote:

> If I had one hour to live, I'd spend it in this class because it feels like an eternity.

Do you think the comment hurt the feelings of the instructor?

*Answer*
Could be. Could be.

We have plenty of advice for professors who are struggling in the classroom. Don't lecture if it does not work. Try something interactive. Don't force the subject matter or materials down the throats of the students. Get some help from other instructors to find out a way to make the class work. If you can't control the class, consider breaking it into groups and let them work on assignments on their own.

All good suggestions. Let's focus on others.

## USING HUMOR TO ENHANCE LEARNING

The following exercise encourages student creativity when presented with PowerPoint slides in a question-and-answer format.

**Question**
If you're going to make a parachute jump, at least how high should you be?

*Answer*
Three days of steady drinking should do it.

**Question**
Back in the old days, when Great Grandpa put horseradish on his head, what was he trying to do?

*Answer*
Get it in his mouth.
    And some classics from Woody Allen.

**Question**
Does Woody Allen want to achieve immortality through his work?

*Answer*
Not really. He wants to achieve immortality by not dying.

**Question**
Woody Allen does not believe in God but would believe if God gave him some clear sign. What does he want?

*Answer*
Woody Allen wants God to make a large deposit in his name in a Swiss bank account.

**Question**
Woody Allen said, "Man kills for food and not only food." What else does he want?

*Answer*
"Frequently, there must be a beverage."

## TIPS FOR USING SLIDES

The most popular software for presentations in college classrooms is PowerPoint. It is easy to use and can be stored offline in personal computers. Prezi allows students to zoom in and out of their presentation media as they display and navigate information. Google Slides allows easy sharing of presentation materials.

Presentation software needs to be used properly. Here are some tips:

- **Information Overload.** Students can only handle a limited number of important ideas at one time. A good guideline is one key point per slide.
- **Word Overload.** You don't need elaborate sentences and lengthy descriptions.
- **Small Print.** It is devastating.
- **Student Literacy.** Do not read the information on the slide.
- **Use Graphics.** A picture is worth a thousand words.
- **Know the Presentation.** Organize the slides to fit your personal style.
- **Put Stories on Slides.** Students will engage from slide to slide looking for the next element in the story.
- **Content Rules.** Do not bog down in fancy templates and design choices.
- **Watch the Slide Background.** The text must be clearly visible.

## PICK THE WINNER OF THE KENTUCKY DERBY

A different classroom activity uses an interactive format to point out overconfidence in critical thinking.

- Students are given information on the horses that were the ten top finishers in the Kentucky Derby in 2012.
- With each horse is information on its prior racing record and an evaluation by a handicapping expert.
- Students are divided into groups and asked to forecast the first place, second place, and third place finishers and provide an estimate of their confidence that they picked the winners.

**Question**
Are students successful forecasting the winners?

*Answer*
No. The outcome is always the same. Few groups pick more than one of the top three horses. Rarely does someone pick the actual winner.

**Question**
Do the students express confidence in their choices?

*Answer*
Totally. Virtually all groups show high confidence in the wrong guesses.

**Question**
What is the goal of the exercise?

*Answer*
Originally it was to teach students to be careful of overconfidence. They think they know things that they simply don't know. This avoids a fatal mistake of the lecture method when we don't take feedback on whether learning is taking place.

**Question**
Is that the only goal?

*Answer*
Other lessons emerged that were not part of the original goal. Some students picked horses with the lowest odds and lost. They did not feel the loss. If the horse had won, a return of three dollars on a two-dollar bet was trivial. Others bet on a horse with high odds. This would produce fewer wins but a single success would be exciting. Such a bet would not be irrational at all.

## A LIVING CLASSROOM

The lesson learned was originally to beware of overconfidence. It added the value of taking a chance. A long shot win is more pleasurable than frequent small wins. Even a long shot loss is something to talk about. These lessons would have little impact if they were presented without student interaction.

The exercise caused one student to use a handheld device to look up the highest odds on a winning horse in Kentucky Derby history. Sent off at odds of ninety-two to one, Donerail paid $184 to win in 1913. This discovery raised the excitement level in the whole class even though it had nothing to do with the exercise. It may help students retain other lessons learned in their long-term memory.

## WHAT DO YOU KNOW ABOUT MCDONALD'S?

Our final interactive exercise improves critical thinking. We start with a written handout. Each team answers questions and expresses the level of confidence it has in its answers.

## McDonald's Handout

Circle each answer and indicate the level of confidence that you chose the correct answer. High, medium, or low.

1. How many people are served daily by McDonald's in the United States?

   28 million        58 million        78 million        100 million

2. Which country's GDP equals McDonald's annual revenues?

   Australia        Belgium        Ecuador        Haiti

3. How many U.S. employees does McDonald's have?

   700,000        1 million        1.5 million        2.5 million

4. Which of the following is the name of the McDonald's clown in Japan?

   Ronald McDonald        Donald McDonald
   Tojo McDonald          None of the above

5. What percentage of Americans once worked for McDonald's?

   12 percent        20 percent        30 percent        More than 30 percent

6. What percentage of the world's people correctly identified the Christian Cross?

   28 percent        54 percent        68 percent        88 percent

7. What percentage of the world's people correctly identified the McDonald's Arch?

   28 percent        54 percent        68 percent        88 percent

8. Who owns a McDonald's near London, England?

   Queen Elizabeth    Bill Gates
   Donald Trump       Lady Gaga

9. What country is second for number of McDonald's?

   Japan              India
   China              United Kingdom

10. Which of the following was done by a McDonald's in Australia to force teenagers to stay off the premises late at night?

    Played            Serves only       Stop serving      Promoted a
    classical music   Chicken           Chicken           citywide teenage
                      McNuggets         McNuggets         curfew

## McDonald's Answers in Bold Type

1. How many people are served daily in the United States?
   **58 million**

2. Which country's GDP equals McDonald's annual revenues?
   **Ecuador**

3. How many U.S. employees does McDonald's have?
   **700,000**

4. How many new U.S. hires every year?
   **Name of McDonald's Clown in Japan. Donald McDonald (Japanese language does not have the sound for the letter "R.")**

5. What percentage of Americans once worked for McDonald's?
   **12 percent**

6. What percentage of the world's people correctly identified the Christian Cross?
   **54 percent**

7. What percentage of the world's people correctly identified the McDonald's Arch?
   **88 percent**

8. Who owns a McDonald's near London, England?
   **Queen Elizabeth**

9. What country is second in number of McDonald's?
   **Japan**

10. Which of the following was done by a McDonald's in Australia to force teenagers to stay off the premises late at night?
    **Played classical music**

## Lessons Learned

As we allowed students to score the questions one at a time, lessons emerged.

### 1. We tend to be overconfident.

Ninety-two percent expressed medium or high confidence on individual answers whereas only 44 percent were correct. Only 61 percent were correct when students expressed high confidence.

### 2. Students have fun when they are engaged.

Prior to identifying correct answers, we chose a scoring system.

- **Right Answer**. One point. This was obvious.
- **Wrong Answer with Low Confidence**. One point. The logic is we should be rewarded when we acknowledge that we need to do more research before answering some questions.
- **Right Answer with High Confidence**. One additional point. The logic is to reward us when we know something and say we know it.
- **Wrong Answer with High Confidence.** Minus one point. The logic is that it hurts us when we make decisions in a display of overconfidence.

Aside from the results, the scoring was quite animated. As each correct answer was announced, it was greeted by either a cheer or a groan. Answers were challenged or disputed by teams that missed them. Both right and wrong answers were supported by the teams that marked them.

In the process, we could detect anger and annoyance. With high confidence on 61 percent correct answers, teams were pleased with two points each. Students soon realized the 39 percent incorrect with high confidence largely offset their success.

### 3. Students sometimes do not like the rules.

A widespread feeling was expressed that it was all right to reward confidence when we got it right but it was not fair to punish people who expressed high confidence when they were wrong.

### 4. We get unexpected classroom results.

The students are not the only ones who can learn in a classroom. Our story continues when we used the McDonald's quiz in a different context. In another experiment, students were previously given a non-McDonald's confidence exercise. They learned the winning scoring system is to always select low confidence.

When the McDonald's test was administered after this lesson is learned in a different earlier test, students divided into two points of view. "Honest Answer" teams select medium confidence when it is accurate even though you can never score a point with it. "Game Players" select low confidence for every answer unless they absolutely, positively, know-for-sure the answer.

**5. We get into discussions of honesty and even ethics.**

Honest players claimed they made an ethical choice for honesty. Game players saw no ethical issue. They are confident they will win and that is what mattered.

This gave us a chance for more learning. When we got to the scoring, we discussed the "winning" strategy and some teams were confident they got it. Then, we pointed out honesty is a pretty good thing so we gave three points for any medium answer. The honest answer teams were thrilled. The game players felt cheated.

**Question**
Success with the McDonald's exercise encouraged us to try another approach. One semester, students took a prior non-McDonald's exam so they learned the winning strategy of always answering with low confidence. Then, we invited another class to compete against us in the quiz on McDonald's. How did that work out?

*Answer*
It created a spirit of competition and camaraderie until the other class realized they were at a disadvantage. Our class knew the correct strategy to win and always answered with low confidence. As we scored the answers, teams from the other class protested. The sentiment was, "You tricked us."

We then discussed how much we hate it when others know the rules and we don't.

## CONCLUSION

Nobody, students and instructors alike, enjoy dull classes. It takes a little extra work to enliven the classroom and enhance learning. New instructors should take to heart that their graduate education did not fully prepare for the role of being an effective instructor.

*Chapter Ten*

# Did You Hear about the Death of Written Exams? Did the End of Cursive Writing Pass You By?

> No need to encrypt our communications. Someday we old people will use cursive writing as a secret code.
>
> —Anonymous

> God grant me the serenity to accept the things I cannot change, the courage to change the things I can, and the wisdom to know the difference.
>
> —Reinhold Niebuhr, theologian and professor at Union Theological Seminary

## COLLEGE AND CAREER READY— STUDENT VERSION

Reform efforts in secondary education seek to improve reading, writing, speaking, listening, and language. Six common core high school standards have been identified.

- **Critical Thinking**. Improve understanding of key points in oral and written communications, request clarifications, ask relevant questions, and effectively explain ideas.
- **Content Knowledge, Comprehension, and Assessment**. Encourage effective reading and listening to understand meaning and assess accuracy of viewpoints and soundness of logic.
- **Emotional Intelligence**. Develop skills for interacting with others.

- **Nature of Evidence**. Distinguish between facts, beliefs, opinions, assumptions, emotions, and bias when reading or listening.
- **Role of Technology**. Enhance skills using technological tools to enhance learning.
- **Tolerance**. Improve efforts to understand other perspectives and cultures and communicate with people of varied backgrounds.

## COLLEGE AND CAREER READY—PROFESSOR VERSION

Do we have similar efforts to develop professors? We could ask graduating seniors to rate their college experience.
**Test for Students:** Professors helped me

- improve my ability to understand key points in oral and written communications;
- read purposefully, listen attentively, and verify or challenge information;
- develop skills interacting with others;
- read and listen to precisely understand and assess accuracy of viewpoints and soundness of logic;
- distinguish between facts, beliefs, and opinions when drawing conclusions from reading or listening;
- enhance my skill using technological tools to acquire and share knowledge; and
- improve my understanding of other perspectives and cultures.

**Question**
What would we learn if we gave this exam to graduating seniors in college?

*Answer*
It depends on whether you ask them to apply it as an aggregate of all or individual professors. In most colleges, the scores would be positive for the overall experience and devastating in terms of a few individuals. You know who they are.

**Question**
If professors do not score well on the exam, can they do anything about it?

*Answer*
Yes. They can apply the common core high school standards to their own teaching.

## IS CURSIVE OBSOLETE?

Many people in the academy rue the "dying art" of handwriting in a typing, texting, and social media world. Grandparents and educators fear and resist the loss of cursive. The American Handwriting Analysis Foundation published "The Truth about Cursive Handwriting: Why It Matters in a Digital Age." It consists of twenty-two pages, supported by eighty-two scholarly references endorsing the benefits of and refuting opposition views to cursive writing.

**Question**
Does anyone celebrate handwriting?

*Answer*
Yes. National Handwriting Day reminds Americans of the joy of penmanship. It is celebrated on January 23, the birthday of John Hancock. This signer of the Declaration of Independence is famously but erroneously known for signing his name bigger than everyone else's so that the "fat old King of England could read it without his spectacles."

**Question**
Does Hallmark make a greeting card for January 23?

*Answer*
Maybe not. People can make their own as shown in figure 10.1.

**Question**
Virginia first grader Anaya Ellick, age seven, had such good handwriting, she beat out fifty other youngsters from around the country to win the 2016 national handwriting contest. Who cares about that?

*Answer*
A lot of us. Anaya was born without hands. Her achievement was precursive with handwriting in print but still impressive.

**Question**
Is nostalgia for cursive handwriting a product of the digital age?

*Answer*
Not exactly. People have long been concerned about children not learning cursive. In 1935, *Time* magazine carried a quote, "Penmanship is sort of dying out."

Figure 10.1  Card to Celebrate January 23rd. *Source*: Tracey Tango

## CURSIVE IN THE CLASSROOM

No matter your view on cursive in general, it is obsolete in the limited arena of the classroom. Two places really.

- **The Lecture.** This format for presenting information to be written down no longer works. It's a waste of classroom time. Put the material on slides and allow students to download them after the lecture. Assign additional reading to take place at the student's own pace.
- **In-class Exams.** During an in-class essay exam, a student can be expected to write about ten words a minute. A two-hour exam can produce about twelve hundred words. This is rarely enough to encompass the material covered in mid-term or final exams.

**Question**
How can we have classroom discussion on assigned topics if the student has not listened to a lecture on the material or read the chapter in advance?

*Answer*
Ask any professor. We do it now.

**Question**
How can we measure enough learning with multiple-choice exams?

*Answer*
We can't. We measure short-term memorization in most cases, perhaps as much as 80 percent of the testing points.

**Question**
How can we measure enough learning with an essay exam at a writing rate of ten words per minute?

*Answer*
We can't. We need to teach professors how to design essay exams to be completed outside of the classroom and submitted electronically during the final exam period.

**Question**
Suppose a school has a mandatory time for the final exam. How can you not use it?

*Answer*
You can. You can assign the paper to be submitted earlier and then use the final exam period to discuss the answers. Some professors use it simply to hold a pizza party and celebrate the end of the term.

**Question**
One of your students turned in a quiz answering the question, "What is the role of the Internet in social relationships today?" What grade would you assign to the following answer?

> Nowadays, one source that many people use is "Internet." Internet is very useful for people there has information. People can search and find anything that they want also people use Internet for contact each other. On the other hand Internet provide opportunity for people and also provide danger because of if people have an important information maybe someone stolen their information, just put the information in a small device. Maybe your important information will discover and effect your company or your organization.

*Answer*
Whatever your answer, would it change if you knew the student was a highly motivated sophomore who learned English in high school after her family moved to Canada from Thailand when she was a senior in high school?

**Question**
Is there any role for cursive writing?

*Answer*
We might ask the same question about the rotary dial telephone, the typewriter, and the need to perform the steps of long division in our math calculations.

## CONCLUSION

Sometimes we make our own purgatory. When the old techniques are no longer working, we need to make changes. Otherwise, we make little progress with the real issues that help the academy fulfill its proper role in a changing world. We can consider what our students need and revise the way we meet those needs. It is a timeless lesson.

*Part III*

# LIFE ON THE FACULTY

*Chapter Eleven*

# How about a Last Great Lecture Just for Posterity? Can You Offer Some Words of Wisdom for the Ages?

> Before I came here I was confused about this subject. Having listened to your lecture, I am still confused. But on a higher level.
>
> —Enrico Fermi

### COMPELLING VISIONS

The pursuit of the presidency in the United States in 2016 offered two candidates with different compelling visions.

- **Donald Trump.** The slogan Make America Great Again was supported by rhetoric to voters who were angry about job losses, other economic uncertainty, high crime rates, and terrorist threats.
- **Hillary Clinton.** Positive slogans included "Stronger together" and "Love triumphs over hate."

Some Americans responded to the message of Mr. Trump. Some to Ms. Clinton.

Somewhere along the way higher education lost sight of a compelling vision. In the 1950s most parents and children knew college was the ticket to a better life. If you were raised on an isolated farm or crowded city street, you could do better. The door would open for a larger home, new car, and family vacations.

College faculty became lax in subsequent decades. Young people were trapped. College was the toll road out. Professors were the toll collectors.

**Question**
Two students completed an honors English course in high school. They went to different colleges. Each requested opting out of a similar college course. The professors who taught the courses had to approve. What did they do?

*Answer*
One suggested taking a more advanced English elective to gain an understanding of college-level critical thinking. The other refused permission with no explanation.

## GENERAL EDUCATION

The first two years of college are usually a series of totally unrelated courses. In the medieval university, it took six years to achieve a master of arts. At the end of four years the university awarded a bachelor of arts. Little has changed in seven hundred years.

**Question**
One apparent difference today is that many liberal arts colleges also require a foreign language. Why was language ignored in the medieval university?

*Answer*
It wasn't. All instruction was given in Latin, a foreign language to all the students. They were required to have a high degree of oral and written fluency.

## THE COMMON TEXTBOOK

The quality of a medieval university could be judged by the size of its library. Prior to 1439, hand-scripted manuscripts stored the world's knowledge, whether in Europe, the Middle East, or Asia. Universities guarded the precious manuscripts and shared them with students. After Gutenberg's invention of the movable type press, books flourished and universities built great libraries.

**Question**
Are professors generally pleased with the convenience of using a textbook written by someone they don't know?

*Answer*
Textbooks have become a controversial issue on several fronts:

- **Cost.** They are purchased by students who are essentially forced to buy them. They are ordered by professors who may not pay attention to price.
- **Content.** They include much more material than can be covered in a course. They work better as a reference book rather than a guide to learning.
- **Usage.** Many professors require but do not make much use of textbooks. They are simply ornamentation for a course.

## THE COMMON ASSIGNMENTS

Courses look a lot alike without producing optimal learning experiences. The class meets for twenty-four to forty-two sessions with lectures and note taking. Some interaction occurs as do written examinations, outside assignments, and short quizzes. Attendance is taken and absences count against the student.

Some instructors pull it off. Some classes feel like a slow death to students.

**Question**
A department chair knows a professor does not prepare for class. He assigns textbook readings, talks vaguely about them, and gives multiple-choice exams provided by the publisher of the text book with answer sheets electronically graded in the computer center. Is this acceptable to the chair?

*Answer*
Could be. If the professor has an active research record, it may offset poor teaching. If the professor has tenure, what can the chair do?

## THE COMMON LECTURE

Rare is the professor who can prepare twenty-five or more interesting lectures for a course. All too often the result is a series of classes that blend one into the others over an academic term. The students feel the pain early. By the end, the professor is suffering also.

There are many ways to break the monotony and many professors use them. Too many do not. The lecture method has a bad reputation.

## Question

A department was having trouble with students doing poorly on exams. It approved a policy that the last class session before an exam would be a review of the material. Is that a good idea?

*Answer*

It depends on the goal. Why is it valuable to cram short-term teaching points into a "night-before-the-exam study session?"

## WHERE IS THE VISION?

Too many classroom experiences are not worthy of Plato's academy or even the medieval university. Classes are mired down in a routine that excites no one, including the professor who is in a rut. Ms. Clinton and Mr. Trump may have different visions but at least they excited their disciples. The professoriate has a lot to learn from the unruly and disappointing 2016 presidential marathon.

Perhaps all is not lost. Let's play with this a little.

## DECORUM IN THE CLASSROOM

Carrie J. Preston was an associate professor of English at Boston University, when she had dinner with colleagues. A question arose, "Do you make your students call you 'Professor'?" Opinions varied by age, gender, and cultural background.

- **Youngish Professor.** Comfortable with informality including a first-name basis with students.
- **Older Professor.** Issue rarely came up as students simply called him "professor."
- **Female.** Students were less respectful to her than to her male colleagues.

The discussion brought back Carrie's memories of her course on the ancient Japanese Noh theater. At the beginning of each lesson, the student performed a customary bow to the professor along with the words, "Thank you for your guidance in this lesson and beyond." After the class started, students always addressed the instructor as "Sensei," a Japanese term that translates literally as "Master."

## Question

After three or four class sessions, a female professor decided to say something about male students who wore baseball caps, some with the brim facing backward, in class. She suggested they remove the caps. Did anyone say, "But of course, Sensei" or its Western equivalent?

*Answer*
Take a guess.

## HONORIFIC GESTURES IN THE CLASSROOM

The modern college class does not promote honorific gestures showing reverence to professors, knowledge, or anything else. This produces three options for professorial behavior:

- **Equality.** The professor and student are just two people on a joint journey. As independent citizens, they can determine their own roles and behaviors.
- **Linear Hierarchy.** The professor is in charge and the role of student is to listen.
- **Respect for the "Sensei."** The professor is respected in the role of "master" and students are respected as the reason for her existence.

**Question**
A professor regularly invites speakers to address his class. The class begins ten minutes before the speaker's arrival. As the individual enters the room, every student rises, walks forward, and shakes hands along with a warm greeting. Is this necessary?

*Answer*
No, but it does two things. The speaker feels welcome and respected, both at the same time. The student makes a personal contact that changes the level of interest in what happens next. Respect for the "Sensei" is also respect for the student.

**Question**
Returning to professor Preston, how does she resolve the issue of decorum in the classroom?

*Answer*
She clarifies upfront that she should be addressed as Professor Preston. Both the "master" and student are likely to be more comfortable knowing the professor brings expertise and authority to the learning situation.

*Chapter Eleven*

# THE LAST LECTURE

We finish with a vision.

> In today's higher education we, the professoriate, pursue a recognition that our goal is to share the knowledge of a "master."

We already acknowledged this does not always happen. Wouldn't it be something if professors and students approached every classroom with excitement and anticipation? This is what happens when we have a real "last lecture."

*The Last Lecture* by Randy Pausch and Jeffrey Zaslow, is a *New York Times* best-selling book. It arose from a challenge to answer the question, "What wisdom would you try to impart to the world if you knew it was your last chance?" Randy Pausch delivered the lecture a month after learning that he had terminal pancreatic cancer. He died ten months later.

The lecture was structured in three components.

- **Childhood Dreams**. The importance of being inspired to dream.
- **Enabling the Dreams of Others**. For Pausch, the achievement of his dreams required him to develop ways to help others pursue their own dreams. He created software that allowed children to have fun while they learned.
- **Lessons Learned**. Among all the things he shared, perhaps the most meaningful was. "It's not about how to achieve your dreams. It's about how to lead your life."

## Mary Kate Naatus

Professor Naatus is a widely respected associate professor at Saint Peter's University. She has a PhD in Global Affairs with a concentration in International Management from Rutgers University. Her dissertation topic dealt with economics in El Salvador where she served in the Peace Corps.

In 2016, graduating seniors invited her to give a "last lecture." The following are highlights of her message with minor editing.

### Childhood Dreams

Dr. Naatus told students she did not fulfill her childhood dreams to be a pilot, a firefighter, or the once-upon-a-time thought that she would have a career in the military. She finished college and found herself doing a stint in the Peace Corps. At least she was earning $200 a month for a few years.

Not bad news at all. The Peace Corps changed her life and apparently led to fulfilling a dream she never had.

She reflected upon the dreams of her own children. When she asks them what they want to be when they grow up, she gets a sense of Disney's influence on their concepts of reality. Her four-year-old wants to be a ninja. The seven-year-old, a policewoman. The ten-year-old, a designer of video games.

Not to worry. The only constant in life is change. It will work out. The Peace Corps was not in the dream. Now she is a professor. Not on the radar screen but a fine choice. When opportunity knocks, answer the door.

## Enabling the Dreams of Others

Professor Naatus is not fully described in her curriculum vitae. Neither does her LinkedIn profile tell the whole story. She enables the dreams of others. How do you tell that to the world? It's in her "last lecture":

> For those of you who are still looking for a position right now, stay active. Volunteer to build a website for a local business or nonprofit. Help out a family member or continue to be involved in your community.
>
> Find your passion and you'll never work a day in your life. The journey starts today.
>
> I feel lucky to have gotten to know so many of you in classes, as student–athletes and campus leaders, as volunteers at community events, and friendly faces walking around campus.

## Lessons Learned

Should a professor limit the understanding of her students to what they do in the classroom or submit in assignments? Nah. Dr. Naatus addressed social media:

> At a time when many of us are debating whether faculty and staff should be interacting on social media platforms, I'm way past that discussion. I connect with my students. It allows me to see a dimension of their lives outside the classroom.

Some of the social media advice involved warnings.

> As your Facebook friend, I saw your posts, even those that might embarrass you in the wrong hands.

She reminded everyone that 70 percent of employers Google applicants before making a job offer. Even after employment, watch out for the dangers of social media.

> If you call in sick to spend a warm summer day at the beach, don't post the photo on your Facebook page.

She believes in knowing the full person.

> Students "come into view as an amazing group of leaders, artists, businesspeople, historians, biologists, journalists, and more."

She sees how they manage their "super busy schedules" that include community service hours, volunteerism, and civic and community engagement. She is reminded once again that they are "amazing."

She learned that being a professor is more than being a subject matter expert. The lecture mixed empathy and wisdom:

> You are finishing up college and moving on. A mix of excitement, relief, and sense of uncertainty about leaving. Whether a job or graduate school, I commend you and wish you the best. Ideally, try to find a job that helps pay for graduate school even as it gives you money to repay college loans.
>
> All along the way ask, "Am I doing something meaningful? Am I learning? Am I connected to other human beings? Do I balance work life and family life?" After you look back in 10 or 20 years, will you be able to say, "I Made a difference."

A last lecture to students can be quite inspiring. What do we say to students who spend day after day with boring instructors and questionable approaches to teaching? Perhaps we tell them they can endure it as part of the overall process of learning about life. Be patient and find the lessons that shape character, values, and behavior. The following story may help understand this point.

### *Father on a Train*

Reader's Digest publishes hundred-word true stories submitted by subscribers. One story from thirty years ago:

> When I was a little boy, my father and I were riding on a train. A conductor berated my father and humiliated him over a minor violation with his ticket. When the conductor left the car, I said, "Why did you let him do that to you?" My father replied, "If that man can live with himself every day of his life, I can live with him for five minutes."

This story might come to mind the next time a student asks you, "Why do I have to put up with that professor's boring lectures?" Five minutes is one thing. A whole semester encourages avoiding the course, transferring to another school, or dropping out of college.

## CONCLUSION

If the professor does have a vision, all is lost. Dr. Naatus described what it means to be educated. The right college experience can raise students to the top of the mountain and help them see and understand distant lands. It is filled with things that matter. Childhood Dreams? Enabling the Dreams of Others? Lessons Learned? What else can we say? Nice job professor Mary Kate Naatus and all the "Sensei" who pursue the same goals for their students.

*Chapter Twelve*

# Should You Be David or Goliath in the Classroom? As Goliath Is My Role Model, What's the Question Here?

It's always better to shock people and change people's expectations than to give them exactly what they think you can do.

—Jonah Hill, author

### BELIEVE IT OR NOT

The story of David and Goliath appears in ancient Jewish, Christian, and Islamic texts showing a triumph of God over infidels. The Philistine and Israeli armies were camped for battle. Goliath, a Philistine giant wearing full armor, challenged the Israelites to send a champion to fight him. David, a young shepherd boy, accepted. Dressed in a simple garment armed only with a sling and pouch of stones, he approached the lumbering Goliath. With a single stone from his sling, David struck a disabling blow and won the battle. When the Philistines saw their hero was dead, they fled. The Israelites pursued, killed them, and plundered their camp.

**Question**
Does a professor in the classroom remind you of Goliath? An intellectually lumbering giant in heavy theoretical armor? Or perhaps David? A lithe combatant, quick and nimble, on the battlefield of ideas?

*Answer*
Perhaps neither. Perhaps both. Everybody has stories from their college and university experiences.

# GLADWELL'S DAVID AND GOLIATH

Malcolm Gladwell's *David and Goliath: Underdogs, Misfits, and the Art of Battling Giants* is a book that, among other things, changes our perception of the combatants.

- **Goliath.** Most people believe David was the underdog. Not true at all. Weighted down with heavy armor and using weapons that required closeness to kill, Goliath was a sitting duck. One rock well placed and Goliath was down. David then closed in for the kill.
- **David.** He was nimble and had a superior firepower. If you don't weigh yourself down, you can move. If you choose the right weapon, you can win.

### Goliath in the Classroom

We meet "Professor Goliath" in the classroom, usually in our freshman year. The Philistines had a single such giant. A university has many.

"Goliath," standing at a podium, obviously a learned person, often a man but not always, introduces a topic unknown to us. Our first humanities, psychology, or philosophy course. We take notes, carefully ask questions, and nervously respond to questions. We fear the battle, often a mid-term exam, perhaps a quiz or written assignment.

### Goliath during the Dissertation

We meet another "Goliath" when he has been assigned, willingly or not, to direct our dissertation. Wearing the heavy armor of a PhD and holding an intellectual scimitar, he stares down the candidate. At each stage—concept, proposal, review of the literature, primary research, findings—he gives us a slice, rip, cut, stab, and poke.

### Goliath in the Hiring Process

As the wounds heal from writing a dissertation, we seek an assistant professorship. It is a daunting task as a hundred or more candidates vie for a single position. Interviews often bring a candidate face-to-face with a lumbering department chair, dean, or search committee.

### Goliath on the Tenure Track

The newly chosen assistant professor, maybe lucky enough to hold a tenure-track appointment, lands amid a bevy of Goliaths. People looking for a fight and believing they are well armed for battle. Be nimble and sling stones? Nonsense. Keep your head down and avoid attracting the attention of a giant.

## Goliath in a Tenured Status

It's not over. It's just the beginning of a battle for recognition, promotion, publication, and acceptance among slow-moving, heavily armed giants and those who aspire to the status.

## Where Is the Academic David?

In fairness, the academy has many nimble and competitive professors of every size and age. They are not encumbered by obsolete practices, ideology, and expectations. They make the academy work in the best traditions of Plato.

## Question

What is the point of the David and Goliath discussion?

*Answer*
We need more Davids and fewer Goliaths in the academy.

## Decision Time

The choice to become a professor will, at some point, force you to choose to follow the model of David or Goliath. Do you want to be nimble and win or bogged down and lose? We can identify specific decision points.

## #1. Choice of a College or University

Of course, we look longingly at Ivy League schools. Who doesn't want to go to a cocktail party and tell friends and strangers they studied or taught at Harvard, Princeton, or Yale? It's not too bad if the reality is Ohio State or the University of Virginia. Nobody wants to identify with Hartwick College. This can be the first David and Goliath mistake.

Gladwell tackles the choice of a college or university for undergraduates but the message applies to aspiring professors. He frames the decision in terms of "big fish, small pond." With 1.5 million faculty members in North American colleges and universities, only a few will rise to the level of big fish. All the others may be disappointed.

Gladwell encourages us to choose nimble over lumbering. Find an environment where you can succeed.

## HARTWICK OR HARVARD?

Hartwick College is in Oneonta, New York. It has fifteen hundred undergraduates and one hundred faculty members. Harvard is, well, you know.

Gladwell profiled science, technology, engineering, and mathematics (STEM) students at both institutions. He used standardized test scores to compare the top, middle, and bottom third of students. He found that the top students at Hartwick had similar scores to the bottom students at Harvard. The top tier at Hartwick was much more likely to succeed than the bottom tier at Harvard. Fifty-five percent compared to 16 percent. Both schools had less than 20 percent success for students in the bottom third (table 12.1).

Gladwell's conclusion? We compare ourselves to those who are around us. A big fish does better in a small pond. Go someplace where you are not the underdog.

### David in the Classroom

Even as we encounter Goliaths on the pathway to becoming a professor, it is not necessarily our destiny to replicate the behavior in our own teaching. We can be nimble. Welcome to Introduction to Teaching 101.

- **The Lecture.** Do not pontificate from a podium. Engage the audience. Make a presentation interactive in a classroom. Employ humor.
- **The Textbook.** Do not assign an eight-hundred-page textbook that cannot conceivably be covered in a single course. If forced to assign a textbook, select chapters you will discuss. Choose materials that are lively, interesting, and useful rather than reference material for late-night reading.
- **The Students.** If they pay no attention, stop talking to them. Give them things to do or questions to answer to move from one-way to two-way communication.

Table 12.1  Comparing Hartwick and Harvard.

|  | Top | Middle | Bottom |
|---|---|---|---|
| Hartwick |  |  |  |
| SAT Score | 569 | 472 | 407 |
| STEM Degree Success | 55% | 27% | 18% |
| Harvard |  |  |  |
| SAT Score | 753 | 674 | 581 |
| STEM Degree Success | 54% | 31% | 16% |

## David in Career Decisions

A similar set of circumstances faces the potential professor making career choices.

- **Tenure Track versus Lecturer.** A newly minted PhD has two offers. One is a tenure-track assistant professor position at a state college. The other is a term appointment as a lecturer at a state flagship university. Which is more attractive? It depends on the conditions. We can't always assume Harvard is more attractive than Hartwick.
- **Two Tenure-track Positions.** A similar individual must choose between identical offers from two private universities. One awards tenure 80 percent of the time while the other awards five-year contracts after a three-year probationary period. Which is more attractive? Once again, it depends.

## Question

An aspiring professor has been accepted into two doctoral programs—American University PhD and Georgetown University Doctor of Liberal Studies (DLS). Both schools require a dissertation for graduation. Which choice will provide nimble opportunities after graduation?

*Answer*

Let's just be honest on this one. The PhD is a better choice. This is the case because many academics are simply prejudiced against any degree other than a PhD. The bias is not even based on reason or actual experience. Either you have a PhD or you don't. No need to explain that individuals with Georgetown DLS dissertations are published in peer-reviewed articles and books on topics as varied as globalization, war and peace, religion, politics, and major events of human history. It makes no difference.

## Question

In the 1960s, the Harvard Business School and others converted PhD programs to Doctor of Business Administration (DBA) degrees. The goal was to reflect a preparation to conduct practical as well as theoretical research. In the 1980s, most of the schools reverted to the PhD. Why the change?

*Answer*

Graduates were being discriminated against because nonbusiness professors did not understand a DBA.

**Question**
Maybe the hiring and promotion and tenure committees properly discriminated against the DBA. They want professors to demonstrate the ability to do research by completing a dissertation. Could that be true?

*Answer*
Nope. The requirements to complete a dissertation were identical for both the PhD and the DBA.
**Lesson Learned:** In many people's eyes, the PhD is the Goliath of degrees.

**Question**
A professor interviewed with New York University and learned the faculty only accepted publications in six journals as qualifying for tenure. An interview with Rutgers provided the same requirements for eight journals. The professor was writing a book that could make a major contribution to her discipline. She would have to suspend the effort to obtain tenure at either school. Why was this a David or Goliath decision?

*Answer*
To attempt to publish work where one has little interest is a choice to be in the bottom third of the pool. Hartwick shows us what happens there.

## CONCLUSION

Perceptions mean a lot and the image of Goliath as the all-powerful and David as the underdog is slow to die. Professors and aspiring professors are advised to understand reality, identify and exploit their advantage, and select the size of their world. This many mean choosing an unreasonable path in the view of others.

*Chapter Thirteen*

# Is the Faculty Search Process Fatally Flawed? Why Do We Make so Many Wrong Hiring Decisions?

I am indebted to my father for living, but to my teacher (Aristotle) for living well.

—Alexander the Great

**BELIEVE IT OR NOT**

An Irish pub in New Jersey was a watering hole for professors from the local university. It was quite "Green" in the sense of being Catholic, and had a dislike for "Orange" representing either Protestants or the British. It was a place of legends for the professoriate but none more memorable than "The Doctoral Incident."

The setting was a Wednesday evening after classes with a group of professors drinking at the bar. Unexpectedly, a patron fell out of his chair and went into convulsions on the floor. Someone shouted, "Is anybody here a doctor?" A slightly inebriated professor at the bar cried out, "Yes. I am a doctor." He ran to the stricken individual and began pounding on his chest.

Some people pulled the "doctor" off the individual. Others attended to the stricken individual and an ambulance took him away. The incident had consequences in the community. The university negotiated a departure of the professor from the faculty.

Perhaps the dean did not consider a doctorate in a liberal arts discipline to be appropriate for a medical intervention.

## THE HIRING PROCESS REVEALED

The formal hiring process for college or university faculty is a perplexing process. When you consider becoming a professor, it may seem straightforward.

- Decide who you are and what you want.
- Check out a bunch of schools and predict what they want.
- Compare your goals with their needs.
- If they match, apply.

**Question**
A doctoral candidate saw an opening for a faculty position requiring intercultural knowledge. It was the exact area of her dissertation. She applied for the job. Who got it?

*Answer*
Someone else who had less qualifications. Seventy-four applications were received by the search committee. One of its members described the hiring decisions: "The major factor in selecting this individual had little to do with the job description. It was just plain luck."

### The Role of Luck

In most academic disciplines, we have too many doctoral-qualified individuals for the available positions. Full-time professorships have been declining in number. The search processes to fill them invite a morass of candidates and qualifications. Luck is often the deciding factor on who gets the job.

### Who Are You?

The hiring process starts with a little reflection.

- **What Do You Want?** Do you want to teach? If yes, do not apply for positions where research is primary.
- **Do You Have a Competitive Edge?** A unique situation based on credentials, skills, or knowledge. If yes, hunt down openings where you have a leg up on others with similar qualifications.
- **Can You Make a Rational Decision?** Do not apply for an opening in Asian History department if your background is Latin American geography.
- **Does Anybody Want Your Profile?** Did you investigate in advance colleges and universities to learn what they are doing about hiring? Odds go up if you assess in advance your chances to be lucky.

## Are You Ready to Take the Journey?

You start by placing initials after your name. Sally Smith, MS or Akash Patel, MA. This is necessary but not enough. From this foundation, a journey begins that has clearly identifiable stages:

- **Apprenticeship.** Graduate school with a PhD or equivalent.
- **Journeyman 1.** The newly minted assistant professor is little more than a trained worker employed by someone else. Success comes from being reliable but not outstanding.
- **Journeyman 2.** After about seven years, promotion to associate professor with tenure. If you are reliable but not much more, this is your ending point.
- **Master.** Promotion to the rank of full professor requires publication in obscure journals. You must pretend they are "works of art" with great value and meaning.

## What Do Schools Want from Professors?

OK. You're not afraid to walk the long road to a professorship. What do colleges expect? Everybody has the same identical faculty handbook.

- **Teaching.** The handbook explains the paramount importance of being effective in the classroom. This is the case even though your application shows no evidence of teaching skills. In some cases, the applicant displays no interest in teaching at all. Neither do the members of the search committee, although they may fake it.
- **Scholarship.** The handbook couches a requirement for research in ponderous terms. This often turns out to be totally misleading as current tenured professors produce mostly pseudo-scholarship. Schools will accept mediocre work, or even nonsense, so you can grind out papers until you get tenure. Only then can you stop pretending.
- **Service.** The handbook describes service in amorphous terms. Get the job. Serve on some committees that sound good even if they require no effort. The academic standards or plagiarism grievance committees come to mind.

In your cover letter and the interview, stress your love for teaching, scholarship, and service. Be sincere, even if you are faking it. Recognize that other factors may be at work to make you lucky. Identify and work them.

## Question
Some search committees only care about the source of your academic degree. What does this do to your chances?

*Answer*

It makes you unlucky if you apply to a "snob" school without a "snob" degree.

Be realistic. Do not apply to a school that values research if you do not have a strong research interest. Do not apply to a department that only teaches lower-level undergraduate courses if you are looking for graduate assistants to help you with your scholarship.

## The Official Hiring Process

Finding and evaluating applicants goes something like this:

- **Curriculum Vitae (CV).** A short account of one's qualifications including education, research, and publications. It is submitted on paper or electronically with a cover letter and an application.
- **Interview and Presentation.** The applicant meets with a committee, dean, and others, and may make a formal classroom presentation to students and faculty members.
- **Criteria.** A search committee evaluates credentials and potential for teaching, scholarship, and service.
- **Offer.** If the individual is successful, the result is a full- or part-time position.

## The Unofficial Hiring Process

The search committee may be pretending to evaluate the standards in the handbook. The real story may lie in "connections." Professors promote their own students to other schools and seek to give them every advantage. They recommend candidates whose interests, talent, and skill do not threaten them or the political balance in the discipline.

## THE ROLE OF CONNECTIONS

People have two types of connections.

- **Strong Connections.** Those with our family, friends, coworkers, and neighbors. We see these people all the time.
- **Weak Connections.** Relationships that are less frequent or even infrequent. They exist with associates at work, neighbors, and other casual acquaintances. We know things about these people but we do not know the people that they know.

The chance to find a faculty position increases greatly if you can work a vast network of weak connections. Professors, classmates, and acquaintances can open doors that they do not know exist. Malcolm Gladwell explains three distinct personalities.

- **Connectors.** People with a special gift for bringing the world together. They can match you with the people they know.
- **Mavens.** Information specialists who pay close attention to details. They can share their knowledge of you and your skills.
- **Salesmen.** Individuals who persuade skeptical people. They can become advocates for your candidacy.

Everybody is a possible connector, maven, or salesperson who, knowing of your goal, could help you find a position.

## Question
All three basic personality types can be found in the academy. Which do you think is the most common?

*Answer*
A lot of mavens are running around. Fewer of the others.

## Question
Of the three personality types, which one contains the people you need to know so they can help you gain an edge in hiring?

*Answer*
Connectors. Mavens can't help you at all. That's not what they do. Salesmen peddle their own activities. They do not sell you. Connectors take pride in bringing together people who connect with them.

## WEAK ALUMNI CONNECTIONS

A woman decided to make a career change. She enrolled in a doctoral program and sought an adjunct teaching position. She became active in the alumni association of her college. At special events, she arrived early, talked with strangers, and made new friends on the faculty. She approached guest speakers, introduced herself, and welcomed them. After the presentation, she engaged the speaker one-on-one and thanked him or her for the words of wisdom.

In many of these encounters she explained her work, her energy, and her ambition to teach. One speaker took an interest in her work. After the presentation, he e-mailed and asked her to call his office. In a matter of weeks, she had an offer to teach a course in the evening school. It was not the area of the speaker who opened the door. He simply knew a department chair looking for an instructor.

People among our weak connections can open opportunities in academia.

## A CONNECTIONS STORY

A master's degree candidate took extra time to discuss course topics before and after class with the instructor. He also described his extensive professional experience. After he graduated, the department had an unexpected vacancy. The instructor recommended him for the course. He taught it and other courses successfully and got to know the members of the Department. When offered a full-time position, he took it. He is now working on his dissertation.

### Question
A new faculty member was in a department with a talented female chairperson. The academic vice president offered her a position in administration. The discussion turned to her replacement. She told the vice president the names of the people in the department. The vice president recognized one person, arguably the least qualified, and chose him to be the new chairperson. What were his qualifications?

*Answer*
The only thing the VP knew was that the individual played basketball with him at lunchtime. A weak connection produced an unexpected outcome.

### Question
Attendance at professional conferences is one of the best opportunities for creating weak connections. An assistant professor was active in the local AAUP chapter. On June 1st, he learned he was denied tenure and would lose his position one year later. Did that happen?

*Answer*
Not exactly. The individual made a few phone calls to AAUP associates and learned of an unexpected resignation at a nearby school. He did not wait a year to leave. He started six weeks later as an associate professor.

## IDIOSYNCRASIES OF SEARCH COMMITTEES

The faculty hiring process is unique in one critical aspect. It involves campus-wide search committees with members who must reconcile different goals and points of view. Some committees are highly productive. Others are virtually dysfunctional consumed by trivial details and unfounded opinions or assumptions.

**Question**
Search committees may include faculty, administrators, and students as members. Do you care if the chair of the committee is a professor, administrator, or student?

*Answer*
Not really. If you are a strong candidate, you hope for a competent chair who can organize a discussion, set an agenda, allow everyone to participate, and control individuals who might dominate or sabotage the search. If you are not particularly qualified, you hope for turbulence and conflict. Sometimes that happens.

**Question**
A professor interviewed for the position of chair of the business administration department at a private university. The search committee had five faculty members, including one representing accounting and one, business law. When it came to their turn, the accounting and law members each asked a modified version of the same question:

> What is your view of faculty members having outside paid employment to enhance their knowledge of the subject matter in the classroom?

What would have been the correct answer for that question?

*Answer*
Whatever the answer, good luck. Many faculty members frown upon professors with opportunities to earn income in extracurricular pursuits. The candidate tried to answer the question to please all members of the search committee. He did not receive an offer.

**Question**
It is not uncommon for schools to require a candidate to conduct a sample class. What happens if you do not prepare something special?

*Answer*
You are flirting with death. The trick is to focus on the audience, not on your subject matter (figure 13.1).

Figure 13.1    Flirting with Death. *Source*: Tracey Tango

**Question**

You are interviewing before a somber group of professors who believe they are serious scholars. What do you do for a forty-five-minute demonstration presentation?

*Answer*

Choose a noncontroversial finding from your own research. Present it in ten minutes. Then, find a way to let them talk. Reality: No one is interested in your work. They want to explain their own thinking about it or something else.

**Question**

Your demonstration audience is a class of thirty undergraduates and three faculty members. It is a fifty-minute class. What do you present?

*Answer*

A single useful insight supported by four to ten slides in a fifteen-minute lecture format. Insert four or more places where you ask a question that is easily answered by the students. Fill twenty minutes with discussions. Finish ten minutes early and thank everyone.

**Question**

What happens if you do not finish at the scheduled time for your presentation?

*Answer*

Nothing good can come from that.

## THE QUALIFIED CANDIDATE

The chair wanted the department to hire a certain person as a new instructor. She knew the individual from professional association meetings and was confident that he would be a fine teacher. She needed recommendations from a search committee with members who often fought in meetings. She scheduled the candidate in separate interviews with each member of the committee with introductions as follows:

- **Professor #1.** He had powerful or well-known acquaintances and was impressed by them. She introduced the candidate as a friend of two U.S. senators. In the entire interview the two men discussed only people that they both knew.
- **Professor #2.** This woman was impressed by research published in academic journals. The man was introduced as the author of articles on cognitive dissonance. The subsequent discussion covered only the mutual research of the two parties.
- **Professor #3.** This man was a rabid fan of the local professional sports team. She mentioned that the candidate was a sports fan. For thirty minutes the individuals discussed football, basketball, and baseball.
- **Professor #4.** This woman was interested in students getting jobs after graduation. The candidate was introduced as a person who worked with employers to find jobs for students when he was doing his graduate work. The discussion involved only this topic.

### Question
After all the interviews, the chair asked each member for a recommendation. They all said the same thing. What was it?

*Answer*
All four professors recommended hiring the candidate for the same reason. The man would be *a good teacher*. The topic of teaching was never mentioned in any of the meetings.

### Question
Colleges often write elaborate job descriptions but the reality is simple. The search committee should only have three concerns about a new candidate.

- Are you qualified to teach and conduct research at the levels we seek?
- Do you want to teach and conduct that research?
- Do we like you?

Of the three questions, which is usually the most important?

*Answer*
In most cases, your academic degree and dissertation are the key to success. Universities hire people they dislike every day. Many of them have no desire to interact with other human beings in any context at all.

## ACADEMIC APPOINTMENTS

Colleges and universities have a relatively standardized approach to adding new faculty. After a search:

- The school will offer a position from a starting to an ending date matching a semester, trimester, quarter, or academic year.
- The contract may be full-time or part-time and may require duties outside the classroom.
- The college will direct the new instructor to read policy documents to learn expectations and confer with the dean or department chair for more information.
- The compensation will be a fixed number with payments spread over the period of the appointment.

The exact appointment will match a category of instructors. If the term adjunct precedes the title, the position will be part-time.

- **Term Appointment.** This contract expires on a specific date and does not renew. Oftentimes, the title does not contain the word "professor." Typical titles are instructor, lecturer, and faculty associate.
- **Tenure Track.** This contract is viewed as the "best" alternative for an inexperienced or unproven professor. Usually a PhD or equivalent degree is required.
- **Tenured.** This is a permanent, continuing status that can only be cancelled for cause. It is a highly desired appointment to say the least, and is rarely given upon hiring, reserved only for unique individuals or those currently holding a tenured position at another school.
- **Visiting Professor.** This is an individual usually from another institution invited to temporarily join the faculty to teach, lecture, or perform research. The invitation is often regarded as recognition of the individual's prominence in an academic discipline, society, government, or field of study.

## Question

A department chair had a late resignation and needed an adjunct professor for a class in German. A colleague suggested a local high-school German language teacher. Is that a qualified person for the job?

*Answer*

Not at first glance, at least in the eyes of the chairperson. True story.

> *Colleague:* I know Janet Chow. She teaches juniors and seniors over at Middletown high school.
>
> *Department Chair:* I don't know her.
>
> *Colleague:* My son is in her class. He thinks she's really good.
>
> *Department Chair:* Does she have a PhD?
>
> *Colleague:* She has a master's degree in German literature.
>
> *Department Chair:* Yeah. That's the problem.

## THE FINAL REALITY

Managing an academic career can be exhausting. In many cases, you have little control over what happens. Tenured professors do not like you or your research. If you are an effective teacher or prolific scholar, you are a threat. Knowledge you carefully cultivated in your doctoral program is of no interest to anyone. You may be the most qualified person for a job but the school has favored candidates ahead of you.

If you get a position, you may be doing a great job. Still, the school may not be granting much tenure. Or, you are getting older and the school wants newly minted PhDs. They cost less and are not so grumpy.

## CONCLUSION

The faculty search process leaves a lot to be desired if it does not produce the right professors to carry out the learning responsibilities of colleges and universities. We have much evidence that it needs to be reformed.

*Chapter Fourteen*

# Is the Faculty Evaluation Process Fatally Flawed? What on Earth Is Going on in That Promotion and Tenure Committee?

Tell me and I forget, teach me and I may remember, involve me and I learn.

—Benjamin Franklin

### BELIEVE IT OR NOT

**Question**
The Promotion and Tenure Committee met to discuss a full-time lecturer who completed five years and could not continue after seven without tenure. The academic handbook was quite specific.

> A professor must have a terminal degree to receive tenure.

The individual taught in criminal justice and had two master's degrees. Teaching evaluations and college service was excellent. What did the committee do?

*Answer*
It voted unanimously in favor of promotion and tenure. The president approved the recommendation even though two master's degrees did not qualify as a terminal degree in the handbook.

## FACULTY ACTIVITIES

It can be complicated to develop an evaluation process to cover every unique combination of faculty activity. Some considerations:

- **Standard Teaching Load.** Most institutions have a base teaching load for full-time faculty members. A typical requirement is eight courses equaling twenty-four credit hours annually.
- **Reduction of Teaching Load.** A school may reduce the required courses. Released or reassigned time encourages faculty members to conduct research or perform administrative tasks or serve on designated committees.
- **Scholarship.** With or without released time, faculty members are usually expected to conduct research and disseminate their findings in the form of working papers or publication.
- **Service.** The faculty member is encouraged to participate in department, college, university, and community activities.
- **Personal Goals and Behaviors.** Professors pursue their interests in the business, political, or social life of the institution.

The role is entirely different for a part-time appointment. Adjunct instructors may be included or omitted in faculty activities based on the whims of the administration or full-time faculty. Some colleges welcome their energy and others ignore them.

The behavior of the part-timer is also shaped by personal motivation. Some individuals simply want to teach. Others want, or even desperately want, to have more involvement.

### Evaluating Teaching

A formal effort is usually made to evaluate performance in the classroom. Efforts include classroom observation by a senior member of the faculty, student evaluations, and a review of the course syllabus and assignments.

### Question

A president of a college met with the chairperson of a visiting accreditation team.

> *Accreditor Chair:* I see you do not conduct formal evaluations of tenured professors. Why is that?

*President:* What's the point? We know we have individuals who are not doing a good job. Why waste the time to document it?

*Accreditor Chair:* You can always start proceedings against incompetent tenured faculty members.

*President:* Really? What would that do?

*Accreditor Chair:* It would allow you to tell everyone that you evaluate all faculty.

*President:* Given the protection around tenure, wouldn't that be a farce?

*Accreditor Chair:* Yes, but it sounds good.

*President:* Good point.

## Student Evaluations

Most colleges and universities have extensive, formal student evaluations of tenured, tenure-track, contingency, and adjunct instructors. The following is taken from a form with a maximum total score of 160.

| Sample Student Evaluation | |
|---|---|
| (sixteen items maximum ten points each) | |
| **Use of Classroom Tools** | 40 |
| Effective use of e-mail and blackboard | |
| Effective use of PowerPoint and videos | |
| Effective use of textbook | |
| Effective use of reading assignments | |
| **Student Relationships** | 50 |
| Grades are fair | |
| Grading criteria is clear | |
| Homework returned on a timely basis | |
| Diverse views respected | |
| Instructor available during office hours | |
| **Teaching Itself** | 40 |
| Learning objectives are clear | |
| Instructor is organized and logical | |
| Teaching includes interactive discussions | |
| Instructor cares about students | |
| **Overall Student View** | 30 |
| This course is challenging | |
| Student recommends course to others | |
| Student recommends instructor to others | |
| **Total Possible Score** | 160 |

## Question
Of the four areas, which do you think is the most important for evaluating effective teaching?

*Answer*
Whatever your choice, the overall student view is less than 20 percent of the total. Does this make sense? Have you ever heard a student say, "What a great instructor! She always meets her office hours."

## Question
Five tenured professors received scores below 50 on the scale of 160. The dean called them in and asked why? What did they say?

*Answer*
Deans have heard a variety of responses over the years.

- "The students lack a work ethic."
- "I won't compromise my attendance policy."
- "These students can't write."
- "These students can't do math."
- "The students are immature."
- "I will not compromise my standards."

## Question
A professor received low student evaluation scores except for the item, "This course is challenging." When confronted by the department chair, the professor explained his high standards caused students to complain. What should be the response of the chair?

*Answer*
Aside from the chair's response, courses are challenging for many reasons. With low student evaluations, a course may be challenging because the instructor in unprepared, disorganized, or has some other impediment that blocks learning.

## Evaluating Scholarship

Academic scholarship refers to research and writing that meet institutional requirements for professional appointment, advancement, and tenure. Four categories:

- **Scholarship of Discovery**. Original research that advances the frontier of knowledge in an academic discipline.

- **Scholarship of Integration.** Synthesizes information across or within a single discipline, across two or more disciplines, or in different systems or time periods.
- **Scholarship of Application.** Takes knowledge from the concepts or theories developed in scholarly discovery or integration and applies them to understand problems or find solutions.
- **Scholarship of Teaching and Learning.** Examines the method and practice of teaching and seeks better approaches to learning.

## Question

A faculty member applied for promotion to full professor. His doctoral degree was in biology but most of his research was focused on biochemistry. He had sufficient publications to meet the scholarship expectation. Did he get the promotion?

*Answer*

No. The P&T committee considered his scholarship to be outside his field and denied promotion. Does a doctorate in biology provide a foundation for research in biochemistry? Apparently only the Lord and P&T committee members know the answer definitively.

## Question

An economics associate professor sought promotion. He submitted extensive publications on the history and politics of Detroit. Was the scholarship accepted by the P&T committee?

*Answer*

No. The research rehabilitating factories, starting up neighborhood businesses, and encouraging small business financing was not suitable for economics.

## Ranking Scholarship

Individual members of P&T committees often disagree on the value of research. Many would accept the following in importance from top to bottom:

- **Scholarly Journals.** Original research accepted after anonymous reviews by other scholars.
- **Professional Books.** Related to the discipline of teaching and research.
- **Professional Trade Journals.** Research on concepts and trends published by associations or professional membership groups.
- **General Interest Publications.** Viewpoints to inform and entertain individuals that may not have expertise in the field.

132                        Chapter Fourteen

- **Professional Working Papers.** Scholarly documents suitable for publishing even though rejected by journals.
- **Conference Proceedings.** Papers presented at scholarly or professional gatherings of scholars in a specific discipline or profession.
- **Book Reviews and Other Writings.** Comments and interpretation of the work of others, opinion pieces, case studies, and similar documents in the discipline.

## Question
A P&T committee was comparing four associate professors. Only one of them could be recommended for promotion. Which one should it be?

- Three scholarly journal articles and a professional book.
- Two scholarly journal articles and three scholarly presentations.
- Two books and one scholarly presentation.
- Six scholarly presentations.

*Answer*
Whatever your answer, every P&T committee will have different views.

## Evaluating Service
Service refers to advising, registration, participation in committees, and other nonacademic duties at the institution or in the community. The college evaluates it based on evidence provided by the faculty member augmented by school records and comments of other parties.

## Question
A professor took twelve years to complete a PhD. His dissertation advisor said, "This is the worst dissertation I have ever seen." After graduation, he took a position and received the lowest student evaluations on the campus. He created no scholarship while on the tenure track. He served on fourteen university committees and participated in all university events. He received promotion to associate professor and tenure. Why?

*Answer*
Could it be that P&T is a political process?

## Question
Bob Campbell came up for tenure review. He got his assistant professorship against all odds because the department chair overlooked the absence of a

doctoral degree. Five years later, still without the degree or any scholarly writing, he came up for tenure. Did he get it?

*Answer*

Yep. A well-liked member of the department, he had no trouble. As one colleague expressed it, "I know he's not qualified. I just can't vote against Bob Campbell."

## SUBTLETIES AND OBSESSIONS

We do not want to finish without a reality check. Significant tongue-in-cheek jargon in academia pokes fun at or explains situations and aberrations in academic life. The following terms show varied perspectives and a sense of humor, even as we address needed changes.

- **Academentia.** The situation when a person or institution in higher education loses touch with all semblance of reality.
- **Accreditation.** The act of certifying that an institution has filled out countless forms, measured elusive things, and filed a formal report with a body that has a limited useful purpose.
- **Adultism**: The rejection of immature, unprepared, and unmotivated undergraduate students and the tendency to ignore, or dislike their presence in a classroom.
- **Advanced Placement Program.** A misguided effort by high school officials to offer courses for university credit.
- **Alternative Education.** Also known as nontraditional education, teaching that's inferior to lecturing.
- **Assessment.** Pretending to document in measurable terms knowledge, skills, attitudes, and beliefs that essentially are not measurable.
- **Blended Learning.** Courses that combine traditionally accepted and validated teaching methods in nonvalidated and trendy experiments.
- **Computer-based Learning.** An educational environment where computers provide peripheral information while professors take a break from the rigors of real teaching.
- **Cooperative Education.** A structured method of offering practical work experience to give students time off from thinking and learning.
- **Integrative Learning.** A theory that explains how two professors who dislike each other can be more successful teaching a course than one professor alone.
- **Medieval University.** An institution in Italy, France, or England in the twelfth century or many U.S. academic entities in 2017.

- **Whackademia.** A conceptual area where institutions and instructors convey the wrong sort of knowledge. It was publicized in the title of a 2012 book.
- **Wisdom.** The ability to learn by remembering everything a professor says and parroting it back on a lengthy examination before you forget it entirely.

## Question
An adjunct faculty member received conflicting information about a course schedule for the fall semester. An associate dean told him he was not scheduled for the course and another instructor was identified in the official course listing. His personal friend, the department chair, told him he would be teaching the course. As it turned out, he did not receive a contract.

A few months later, a problem arose. Although the man was not teaching, he had to deal with an incomplete grade from a course he taught in the prior year. A student with a medical problem finally completed the work and asked him to post a grade. Still angry at the college, the instructor refused. Six months later he contacted the department chair asking to teach a course. Is this an example of "academentia?"

*Answer*
It sure sounds like somebody lost a sense of reality. The school denied the request.

## REWARDS AND RECOGNITION IN THE ACADEMY

Because of few great successes, the academy creates a competitive culture that produces aberrant behavior for recognition and perks.

## Question
A university offers a monthly "Celebration of Faculty Scholarship Luncheon." A professor is invited to share the findings from a scholarly paper that he hopes to publish. Is this a form of reward or recognition?

*Answer*
Sort of. Still, look around the room. Is anyone celebrating the person or his work?

## Question
A dean approved $600 to cover 50 percent of travel expenses for a professor to present a paper at a professional conference. The individual participated as

one of five panel members, each of whom had ten minutes to share findings. Seven other professors formed the audience listening to presentation. Is this a form of reward or recognition?

*Answer*
Sort of, notwithstanding the reality that many conferences accept all submissions because colleges will only subsidize travel when a professor is presenting.

**Question**
A university recognized professors who have completed years of full-time service. For the twenty-fifth year, the professor could choose from a stemless wine glass set, a man's or woman's fleece jacket, or a mantle clock with an inscribed university seal. Are these forms of reward or recognition?

*Answer*
Sort of, particularly if you are drinking wine from paper cups, experience cold in your home in the winter, or have no way to tell the time when you are sitting in front of your fireplace.

## CAUTION IS ADVISED

You would not jump off a cliff into dark water without gathering evidence of the likely depth of the pond. A new professor is advised to investigate how the college or university weighs teaching, scholarship, and service in its evaluation processes. The faculty guide is merely a first-cut effort to understand what happens.

At the department level the same situation exists. Individual members have varying views on who should join their ranks.

After making these assessments, compare the real standards with your own capabilities and interests. A strong researcher may lag in the classroom and an individual who provides extensive service may be unable to create serious scholarship. You know who you are, but do others value what you do?

Finally, how serious are the obsessions at your school? If you cannot deal with them, move on if you have the option.

## MISCONCEPTIONS OF FACULTY EVALUATIONS

*The Chronicle of Higher Education* asked professors:

What is the biggest misconception that academics have about higher education?

The following slightly edited quotes often apply to faculty hiring, appointment, promotions, and long-term retention.

> You think the university is about scholarship and education. It's not. Elite universities are real-estate ventures and investment portfolios, with an educational operation on the side. Non-elite universities are about punching the clock and trying to get the kids through.

> You think academics should put their heads down and things will get better. They won't. We need unified activism now.

> You believe your responsibility is limited to your discipline and not also to the overall educational purpose of the institutions. Bad mistake.

> You don't think you need to prove your worth to the larger society. We always had to do so, and never has the effort been more important than now.

> Some academics teach as if their job is to train students to be professors like themselves. This shows a narrow understanding of the purpose and potential of higher education.

> Many academics believe that their hard work will be rewarded and recognized on its own merits. They tend not to appreciate the fluctuating, market-driven aspects of how work gets valued.

> It is nonsense to believe that higher education will continue to survive in something like its current form for the next 50 years and longer.

> You are wrong when you believe that only one kind of intelligence matters.

> Too many professors think higher education operates according to its own internal logic rather than the social, economic, and political forces shaping the rest of the world.

> You do not get it if you believe college is immune to the forces of the economy.

> Too many faculty members think they are the most important factor in the learning experience of students. Wrong. Their peers are.

## CONCLUSION

The evaluation process for faculty members can be a complex, frustrating, and disheartening process. So much is at stake and so many factors play a role shaping the path from hiring to long-term appointment.

*Chapter Fifteen*

# Should You Do a Stint as Department Chair? Does Anybody Need This Grief?

> Lost causes are the only ones worth fighting for.
>
> —Clarence Darrow, lawyer

The Beatles released a song titled "You Know What to Do." This often applies to the department chair. The challenge is whether you have the desire, authority, or power to do it.

## BELIEVE IT OR NOT

A department chair was in the final stage of hiring to fill a faculty position. One of the candidates had appropriate credentials but the answers to questions at the interview were unsettling. The chair decided to call the individual's current department chair who was not listed as a reference.

*Hiring Chair:* I just have a few questions on Professor Walker, an applicant for a position with us.

*Current Chair:* I know about that.

*Hiring Chair:* Can you tell us anything about him?

*Current Chair:* My university only allows me to confirm employment. We cannot give any other information.

*Hiring Chair:* OK. Nothing else, huh?

*Current Chair:* No. Well, maybe something else. I have a question.

*Hiring Chair:* Sure.

*Current Chair:* Are you familiar with the term, "spaced-out drug freak?"

*Hiring Chair:* Yes, I am. Thank you very much.

## Question

A chair was responsible for certifying that a student completed all required departmental courses for graduation. The registrar sent him the application for graduation. It showed that the student completed the correct ten courses at another school before transferring in his senior year. Reluctantly, the chair approved graduation.

Subsequently, the dean sent an e-mail to the chair with copies to the registrar and student:

> This student failed to take courses at our university and cannot receive a degree from your department. Please inform the student.
>
> This is quite embarrassing. I see that the student is a member of your department's honor society. I expect you to monitor this kind of situation in the future.

What do you do?

*Answer*
You know what to do. Or do you? Is it just another day on the campus for a department chair?

## Question

A student went to the registrar and handed her requested courses for the next term. She learned the bursar blocked her from registering for courses because of a failure to pay a fine for an overdue book from the library. She went and paid the fine but the blockage remained for the next three days. During that time, two of her courses closed because of registration limits. She asked the department chair for help. What did the chair do?

*Answer*
No suggested answer. Just another day on the campus.

## Question

A student needs the signature of her faculty advisor to register for courses. The advisor has not been holding office hours. Another student is protesting a grade. The instructor told him the lower grade was given because, "You talk too much in class." A part-time instructor said he will not teach a course that starts in three days if he does not get more money. What should the chair do?

*Answer*
No suggested answers. Just other day on the campus.

## Question
The retirement of a senior member of the department means the most desirable faculty office is now available. Four professors requested it. You are the chair of the department. What do you do?

- **Professor #1.** The senior person in terms of years in the department.
- **Professor #2.** A former dean who returned to the faculty.
- **Professor #3.** The holder of an endowed professorship recognizing as a leading scholar in the field.
- **Professor #4.** A rising scholar who is being recruited by other universities.

*Answer*
You know what to do. Or do you? Whatever the decision, three or more people will not agree with it. One chair may have figured it out. He refused to do anything. The office stayed vacant until the dean made a decision.

## Question
A department chair received the following e-mail from the dean referring to a tenured professor. How do you respond?

> Three students came to my office and complained that Professor Duncan, their advisor, refuses to meet with them to sign their registration forms. Please fix this.

*Answer*
You know what to do. Or do you?

## Question
A student needs SOC385 Sociology of Deviant Behavior to graduate. The university no longer offers the course and has not identified a substitute for it. The department chair approved a criminal justice course CJU314 Crime, Law, and Deviance as a substitute. The Registrar rejected it. What do you do?

*Answer*
You know what to do. Or do you?

## Question
You are the department chair. The local mayor wants to teach a political science course. The president asked the dean and the dean asked you to schedule the mayor. The professor who would be bumped from the course has threatened to file a grievance against you. What do you do?

*Answer*
You know what to do. Or do you?

140                          *Chapter Fifteen*

**Question**
The students in your department have low scores on a graduate school admissions test. The dean wants you to do something to raise the scores. What do you do?

*Answer*
You know what to do. Or do you?

**Question**
You are told to schedule half of the professors for courses on Monday, Wednesday, and Friday. The other half are on Tuesday, Thursday, and Saturday. Nobody volunteered to teach on Saturday. What do you do?

*Answer*
You know what to do. Or do you?

**Question**
The dean asked you to take a three-year appointment as department chair. The position is accompanied by a stipend of $3,000 and teaching load reduction of one course a year. You estimate your personal time to teach and support one course is 180 hours. The annual time spent on chair duties would be 600 hours. Do you accept the position?

*Answer*
You know what to do. Or do you?

## WHAT IS A DEPARTMENT CHAIR?

At some point in a career, a professor almost always considers accepting an appointment or election to be the chair. The chairman is the highest officer of an academic department. The person is typically appointed by the dean after election or recommendation from members of the department. The chair makes individual academic decisions affecting students, presides over department meetings, and represents the department to the outside world.

Many professors choose life in the academy to avoid tasks associated with management, defined roughly as dealing with people issues. It is not the gig they signed up for.

Too late. Somebody must do it. Faculty members do not want the chair to be someone who does not understand the role of a faculty member.

Does the chair need special characteristics to be successful? Management theory helps answer this question.

## #1. Social Style

Social style builds upon two opposite behaviors:

- **Assertiveness.** In new situations, the individual seeks information or quickly gives direction to others.
- **Responsiveness.** The individual reacts appropriately or sympathetically in personal relationships.

The combination of assertiveness and responsiveness produces four styles of behavior.

- **Analytic.** Pursues accuracy, logic, and consistency. Wants the correct answer and does not engage easily in new personal relationships.
- **Driver.** Wants to get things done. Hates delays. Does not build personal relationships. Needs to be in control in all situations.
- **Expressive.** Uses unlimited energy to explain visions and exciting activities. Gets people excited. Loves others if they share his visions.
- **Supportive.** Understands feelings and builds relationships. Conscious of getting tasks done with people. Shows a genuine concern for the problems of others. Ignores delays.

*Versatility*

Versatility refers to the ability to behave appropriately in different situations. It is independent of any one style.

## Question

A tenure-track faculty member has poor student evaluations and a reputation for assigning more than the average number of course assignments. He also gives more C, D, and F course grades than other department members. How will a chair react to this situation? Answer: A chair will act based on social style.

- **Expressive.** Sit him down and help him understand we are here to help students grow and develop. Excessive coursework and tough grading get in the way.
- **Supportive.** Emphasizes the good features of his teaching, including the positive features of hard work and high standards.
- **Analytic.** Prepares a written evaluation listing student comments while ignoring hearsay and rumors.
- **Driver.** Tell him the truth. Too much work and tough grading turns off students and endangers chance for tenure.

*Backup Style*

Each social style has a different backup style when the pressure gets too great:

- **Expressive Attacks.** Becomes visibly angry and abusive.
- **Driver Becomes Autocratic.** Becomes overbearing and displays anger leading to abuse.
- **Supportive Yields without Protest.** Gives in to the viewpoint of others and becomes silent, seeking to preserve the relationship.
- **Analytics Avoid.** Withdraws and refuses to work toward resolving a tension-producing situation.

## Question

A sabbatical is a period of paid leave granted to a college teacher for study or travel. A chair received five requests from department members and recommended all of them to the dean. Only one was approved. The four unsuccessful individuals reacted per their backup style:

- **Analytic.** No response was sent.
- **Driver.** "Enough is enough. This institution does not appreciate great research and it never will. This means war."
- **Expressive.** "That's all you could do? The dean is a jerk. Neither of you can match up to half the quality of my research."
- **Supportive.** "I am disappointed but thank you for trying to help."

## #2. Management Style

Every person has a basic management style.

- **Hands-off Manager.** Gets the job done through independent and motivated people working together with little interference.
- **Task Manager.** Gets the job done by a group dependent on the manager.
- **Hands-on Manager.** Gets personally involved with the project to be done. Others stand by in case they are needed. Excellent crisis manager.
- **Team Manager.** Seeks personal satisfaction of subordinates. Has less concern for tasks.

## Question

A university is converting four classrooms into faculty offices. It asked the department chair to help design the space. The chair asked four other chairs what he should do. The suggestions:

- **Hands-off.** "Form a committee and let them make the decision. No need to get involved."
- **Task.** "Form a committee, chair it yourself, and steer it."
- **Hands-on.** "Prepare the design yourself and ask for comments from everyone."
- **Team.** "Talk with everyone so all members are satisfied with the recommendation."

*Purpose of Meetings*

Management style is often most visible at department meetings. We hear complaints from faculty members. "We have too many meetings." "We have too few meetings." "We have too short notice on meeting times." "We do not know the purpose of meetings."

## Question
The management style of the chair shapes the meeting:

- **Hands-off.** Does not follow daily activities of faculty members. A meeting is an update on what everyone is doing.
- **Task.** Calls meetings to address specific activities and problems.
- **Hands-on.** Uses meetings to set priorities and assign tasks.
- **Team.** Uses meetings to share ideas and help others.

*Advance Preparation for Meetings*

The chair's management style affects how she prepares for meetings.

- **Hands-off.** Does not do much. Monitors what people are doing.
- **Task.** A lot of preparation. Wants to know specific progress and give guidance.
- **Hands-on.** Considerable preparation. Wants information to be intimately involved with what is going on.
- **Team.** Almost nothing done in advance. Calls a meeting to share what everybody is doing.

*Weaknesses of Management Styles*

Each style has its own weaknesses.

- **Hands-off.** May fail to monitor success or failure.
- **Task.** Does not motivate people to work independently or make decisions.

- **Hands-on.** Does not delegate.
- **Team.** Relies too much on the wrong people.

## #3. Communications Style

Every person has a basic communications style.

- **Two-way Communicator.** Warm and open. Excellent rapport with subordinates. "She is honest and listens to me."
- **Outward Communicator.** Blunt. Does not consider the feelings of others. "You always know where he stands."
- **Intellectual Communicator.** Respected but cold and even remote. Calculating. "Stay out of her way."
- **Inward Communicator.** Empathetic and earnest listener but uninvolved. "He listens but never complains."

## Question

The university president told the department chair that he must hire as a full professor a person who is politically connected to the governor. The chair explains the situation based on communications style.

- **Two-way.** "Well, we have a problem. It is important for the university to hire a person that needs to become part of our community. I need your support on this one."
- **Outward.** "We have no choice. We recommend this hire. I don't want a lot of grief on it."
- **Intellectual.** "It's simple. The hiring will take place. The university makes this kind of decision."
- **Inward.** "I don't know what to do. We kind of don't have a choice. No good can come from fighting this."

## #4. Decision-making Style

Every person has a basic decision-making style.

- **Speedy.** Some people make decisions quickly. They need to be careful to gather enough information.
- **Deliberative.** Others take more time. They need information before deciding.

**Question**
The university asked a chair to propose a concentration in Southeast Asia studies. The responses are based on decision-making style.

- **Speedy.** Do it. This is a rapidly developing area for international commerce.
- **Speedy.** It could be good. Call the embassy and ask alumni what they think.
- **Deliberative.** Appoint a task force of department members to look into it.
- **Deliberative.** Bring the matter to the Faculty Assembly for a recommendation.

*The Successful Department Chair*

The chair is more likely to do well when she recognizes styles, the need for versatility, and the culture of the department and school. Suggestions:

- **Goal.** Get the job done by consensus whenever possible.
- **Delegation.** Let others do the tasks they can do well.
- **Concern for the Task.** Recognize the need for moderation in all things, including time and intensity.
- **View of Subordinates.** Be realistic but do not assign tasks they cannot do.
- **Strength.** When change is needed, be a leader. When stability is the goal, be a manager.
- **Problem-solving.** Look for ideas, talent, and energy everywhere and apply best practices to achieve goals.

## CONCLUSION

Maybe a person wants to be a department chair. Maybe not. A professor who accepts or considers it is helped by an understanding social style, versatility, management style and communications styles, and processes for making decisions.

*Part IV*

# PROTECTING WHAT WE HAVE

*Chapter Sixteen*

# Does a Liberal Arts Foundation Protect Anything That Needs Protecting? What Are We Teaching and Why Do We Teach It?

### BELIEVE IT OR NOT

An accrediting body threatened to withdrew its approval of the curriculum for a specific program. The college faculty met to discuss adding a mandatory course demanded by the accreditors. It soon became evident that an existing course had to be dropped as a requirement in the core curriculum.

**Question**
The discussion focused on dropping one of the two philosophy courses or one of the two history courses. What were the merits of each possibility?

*Answer*
Who cares? Neither department could stomach losing a required course. The subsequent discussion was mostly incoherent.

**Question**
What happened?

*Answer*
The philosophy department had fewer voting members and a smaller number of friends on the faculty. A vote of the faculty assembly removed its course.

**Question**
What does this illustrate?

*Answer*
The possibility that politics, not logic, plays a dominant role in managing an academic curriculum. Never ask a barber, "Do I need a haircut?" Never ask a professor, "Should we keep your course as required for all majors?"

## THE LIBERAL ARTS

For many professors, a liberal arts education is the hallmark of a learned person. Is a graduate of Oxford, Harvard, or the University of Paris more educated than a blacksmith, computer programmer, or electrical engineer? Most academics, but not necessarily those in the science, technology, engineering, or mathematics (STEM) areas, answer "yes" to this question.

The liberal arts originated in Ancient Greece as the knowledge and skills needed to take an active part in citizenship. In medieval universities, it comprised seven areas obscurely known as the trivium and quadrivium. The three lower-level subjects were grammar, rhetoric, and logic and the four upper division areas were arithmetic, music, geometry, and astronomy. Today, liberal arts can refer to academic subjects or overall degrees. Sometimes we think it matches a bachelor of arts degree while a bachelor of science refers to a professional, vocational, or technical curriculum. This distinction does not stand up well to scrutiny. For a degree such as economics, a university may award a BS or a BA degree. Some universities give students the choice of either.

## GENERAL EDUCATION

The first two years of college generally require a program of general education. It covers a common cultural heritage that is a modern version of medieval liberal arts and sciences. Professors agree on the concept of general education but disagree on what it should include. Requirements essentially evolve in silos where departments battle to get their courses included. Outside forces and sponsors weighed in. A college supported by a religious body might have two philosophy and two theology courses. A secular institution might have social responsibility and community service.

## AACU General Education Outcomes

A strategy to revise general education is offered by the Association of American Colleges & Universities (AACU). It created tools to measure sixteen learning outcomes in three categories:

- **Intellectual and Practical Skills.** Ten areas of inquiry and analysis, critical thinking, creative thinking, written communication, oral communication, reading, quantitative literacy, information literacy, teamwork, and problem solving.
- **Personal and Social Responsibility.** Five areas of local and global civic engagement, intercultural knowledge and competence, ethical reasoning, foundations and skills for lifelong learning, and global learning.
- **Integrative and Applied Learning.** A single area to help students make connections across curricula.

## Southern New Hampshire University

Paul LeBlanc, president of Southern New Hampshire University (SNHU), took office in 2003 when the school was oriented toward culinary arts, business, and criminal justice programs. It served 2,500 students and was a modest success.

## Question
SNHU had a minor presence in distance learning. Mr. LeBlanc and the faculty recognized technology and social trends were changing the landscape for higher education. LeBlanc explained, "We want to create the business model that blows up our current business model ... if we don't, someone else will." What happened?

*Answer*
LeBlanc and the faculty developed and delivered distance learning in the right context of offerings. By 2016, more than fifteen hundred students were enrolled in one hundred graduate, undergraduate, and specialty-skill programs. This compared to fewer than three thousand students registered on campus.

## Lemann on General Education

Nicholas Lemann, a Columbia University professor, argues that general education needs to be radically revised. He identifies a suite of intellectual skills that "would empower a student ... to understand information across a wide range of fields ... over the long term."

Lemann limits the application of his concepts. The revised general education does not apply to students who need remediation. He omits graduates with weak writing and math skills, whether because of underperforming high schools or lack of intellectual capacity of the student. It does not apply to vocational training that leads to near-term employment.

Lemann believes an educated person should be able to identify bad or incomplete information, avoid obvious misunderstandings and errors, and operate with confidence in new situations. General education should help build those capabilities.

Lemann's formulation of a general education contains eight courses.

*Information Acquisition 101*

Where do we go to separate beliefs, facts, assumptions, opinions, emotions, and bias? What makes up usable information? How do we distinguish whether academic, documentary, journalistic, governmental, and media information is true or false, reliable or questionable?

*Cause and Effect 101*

How do we use the scientific method to find relationships? As an example:

- **Problem Statement.** Why do children in rural areas of India do poorly in school?
- **Hypothesis.** Children do poorly because they are not being fed properly at home.
- **Testing.** What data exist or could be developed to see if better-fed rural students perform at higher levels than less-fed students?

*Interpretation of Written Meaning 101*

How do we approach written content to identify and understand what it means? Students search for the obvious, the subtle, the hidden, and the missing. Start with a passage in the constitution, bible, or a novel. What does it say? What is its meaning? What does it imply? What can we infer?

*Numerical Literacy 101*

What are the skills we need with numbers to make sense out of them? What insights are not visible in the raw data? Examples could come from polling results, sports statistics, stock market indicators, and government economic data. What are the sources of numbers, who generates them, why do they do it, and what do the numbers mean?

*Personal Perspectives 101*

What do you believe about yourself and your world? Why do others disagree with you? Why is it so difficult to display tolerance, respect, and understanding when challenged by the ideas and behavior of others?

*Visual Language 101*

How do we develop and process information in the form of graphics instead of text or numbers? How do we use visual information to create positive responses?

*Thinking in Time 101*

How do we understand the things that already happened and apply them today? Students examine past events and insert themselves into the situation. What was done? What would they have done? What should be done? What behaviors would produce better or worse outcomes?

*Argumentation 101*

How do we take positions, draw conclusions, and explain our beliefs to others, particularly in confrontation with other viewpoints? What makes a compelling argument? Examples use oral back-and-forth debates and written presentations supported with graphics.

## CONCLUSION

The liberal arts foundation of colleges and universities is likely the explanation of the success of Western society. It is being eroded by a failure to make reforms. The consequences are one factor in the struggles of the professoriate.

## Chapter Seventeen

# Does Anybody Believe in Hybrid and Distance-Learning Courses? Is a Changing World Your Friend or Your Enemy?

> The challenge is ... to change our fundamental views about effective teaching and learning and to use technology to do so.
>
> —Donald E. Hanna and associates

### BELIEVE IT OR NOT

In March 2013, Lewis Duncan, president of Rollins College, addressed the assembled faculty in a sobering speech describing online learning as a viable replacement for traditional courses. He said:

> [W]e are experiencing a "Copernican moment." The college campus is no longer at the center of the education universe.

The faculty response to the presentation was negative. Six days later, the arts & sciences faculty voted no confidence by a margin of sixty-seven to ten. One viewpoint:

> I don't think the way you deal with that situation is by immediately saying we need to toss out everything we've been doing for 50 years.

**Question**
Did Dr. Duncan win his battle with the faculty?

*Answer*
No. In May 2014, Mr. Duncan resigned as president. He subsequently became the provost at the U.S. Naval War College.

## IAN LAMONT ON THE CLASSROOM

Ian Lamont is the founder of an electronic publishing company that created a series of thirty-minute learning guides. In contrast to the material he distributes, Mr. Lamont is an advocate of the in-person classroom. His quotes show his concern about distance learning.

- "I am skeptical that distance education is a substitute for live classroom discussion."
- "The most effective learning takes place in the classroom, where you can easily raise your hand, engage in spontaneous discussions … or approach the professor after class."

Many people agree and even applaud Mr. Lamont. Why? Because we have experienced the excitement, even pleasure, when a superstar professor engages us in a classroom. We walk out exhilarated at the new knowledge, insight, or reflection. Some personal favorites:

- **University of Pennsylvania.** A history professor compared Russia to the bear that must protect her cubs because she has no natural boundaries while the United States is the whale protected on both sides by large oceans. Understand the situation, explain the behavior.
- **Stetson University.** An honors class used the novel *Catch-22* to show how humor can present madness as the way to get across a message of tragedy. Innovate the story, hook the reader.
- **Stetson University.** A history professor explained how China was ripe for communism. A communal mentality with central organization was needed throughout history to produce enough food, fight pestilence, sandbag fields against raging rivers, and protect the nation from ravaging outside armies.
- **George Washington University.** A finance professor showed why cash flow trumps accounting in business. Accounting, boring. Cash flow, wow!
- **George Washington University.** An economics professor showed an understanding of microeconomics as the foundation of critical thinking for how businesses succeed. There is a real value to understanding what economists do. Who knew?
- **Academy of National Economy (Moscow).** A sociology professor showed that personal ownership of property is more important than communal efforts to improve industrial efficiency.
- **University of International Business and Economics (Beijing).** A sociology professor explained how struggle sessions are a key ingredient to

resolving conflicts in Chinese history. Understand the psyche, find a way to communicate.
- **Saint Peter's University.** Mary Kate Naatus explained how the right education leads to self-fulfillment and service to others.

## FAILURE OF TRADITIONAL METHODS

The classroom experience that we remember so well is offset by a host of other situations where it did not work out so well. Examples abound.

### Business Mathematics Class

Taught by an aging math professor, the class always started with a roll call of attendance. Then the instructor would ask, "Are there any questions on the exercises?" Hands would go up, "Can you show us how to do number three?" The professor would turn to the board and start writing. Five or more minutes later, he would turn and ask again. Three or four times, and class would be over.

No one was learning anything.

### Question
If no one learned anything, how did anyone pass the course?

*Answer*
The professor gave open-book tests requiring answers to the exercises in the book. Students completed the exercises in the margins of the text in advance of the test. The answers were copied from the book to the exam paper during the test.

**Caveat:** Over the years it was not necessary to solve the problems. Instead, students purchased used books from prior classes where the answers were already hand-written into the books.

**Lesson Learned:** The price of a used book was commonly higher than the price of a new book. Customers pay more for a more valuable product.

## CHALLENGES TO WHAT WE BELIEVE

From Plato's academy to present day, we hold cherished beliefs about professors.

- **Correct Belief.** The traditional learning process in the hands of the right professor and in the context of the right knowledge is remarkable to say the least.
- **Incorrect Belief.** The traditional model does not fit every situation.

**Question**
What is a question you should never ask an alcoholic?

*Answer*
Would you like a drink?

**Question**
What is a question you should never ask a long-term tenured professor?

*Answer*
Are you doing a good job in your classroom?

## REALITY OF TRADITIONAL METHODS

A starting point for challenging our beliefs on higher education is to look back in history.

### Chinese Meritocracy

As early as 1000 BC, China was a thriving culture with a significant educational component. A hierarchical socioeconomic system ranged from top to bottom with warriors, farmers, craftsmen, and merchants. Over time the warrior class evolved into a bureaucratic scholarly elite. Social advancement depended on passing rigorous, even daunting, examinations.

The learning foundation produced ancient China's advanced science and technology often linked to the "Four Great Inventions" of gunpowder, papermaking, printing, and the compass.

### Plato's Academy

In the fourth century BC, the academy in Athens replaced the rigorous memorization of the Chinese system with new ideas about art, literature, justice, politics, education, family, friendship, and love. The classical Greek model created the foundation for Western philosophy, science, politics, religion, and economics.

The Greek model was kept alive under the Roman Empire until 500 AD or so. Higher forms of learning declined dramatically during the next six hundred years in the so-called Dark Ages.

### Medieval Universities

These institutions largely employed a "tutorial system" in addition to classroom lectures. Faculty "fellows" met weekly with students in small discussion groups to evaluate, defend, oppose, or critique the ideas of others as well as their own. The outcome is learning that is highly authentic and difficult to replicate in a large lecture hall.

Tutorial education exists today. The uninitiated sit at the feet of the master and engage in a dialogue. Some students, let's call them the "fortunate few," study or teach at Cambridge or Oxford in the UK or Williams or New College (Florida) in the United States. Many more participate in variations of the system in private colleges and universities or honors programs in public institutions.

The availability of a tutorial system leads us through a thought process.

- **Our Belief**. It is a superior method to create learning.
- **The Fact**. There is no way we can afford it for all the people who would benefit from it. Nor are there enough professors who have the skills to succeed at it.
- **Our Feeling**. The situation is sad.
- **Our Opinion**. Yes, it is.
- **Our Assumption**. Well, somebody should be able to do something.
- **The Reality**. It's not going to happen.

The lecture is a modification of the tutorial to handle larger groups of students at one time. We are all familiar with it. Thus, the stage is set to discuss hybrid and distance learning.

## IN-PERSON, HYBRID, AND ONLINE COURSES

Leaving behind the history, we have three primary formats for higher education today:

- **Traditional.** Students sign up for courses taught just like those in elementary and high school. They enter a class and sit down. An instructor stands at the front of them and talks. Lecturing, questions and answers, group projects, and other interactions provide knowledge. The student completes exams or assignments to receive a grade.
- **Online.** The instructor and students do not meet in person, except perhaps at the start or during exams.
- **Hybrid.** The same as the traditional format, except fewer class meetings. The instructor assigns additional work to be done outside of class.

### Components of Online Course

Distance learning has been around for more than fifty years with the same four basic elements:

- **Learning Management System (LMS).** The infrastructure once were the telephone, post office, printed textbook, or supplemental materials such as study guides. Today it is the Internet, e-books, videos, and interactive-learning software.
- **Content.** A wide range of Internet resources augment the LMS. Students listen, read, or watch on their own schedule. Instructors set up discussion groups or other interaction at specified times.
- **Assignments.** Most courses require written assignments, posting submissions to discussion boards, or participation in discussion groups. Group projects may be assigned and group meetings may take place using Skype or Go to Meeting.
- **Grading.** Instructors assess student achievement with formal tests, submitted assignments, and participation in online discussions.

## Question
How serious is the problem of cheating in an online course compared to a traditional classroom?

*Answer*
It depends upon who you ask. Instructors who oppose distance learning often believe cheating is rampant. To them, it just seems logical that it must be. Experienced online instructors recognize it happens but that is also true for traditional courses.

## Question
How serious is the problem of getting students to "do all the work" in a distance learning course?

*Answer*
The problem seems to be about the same as with a traditional course. The instructor tries to make students appear, either in the classroom or online. The value of the activity varies greatly in both environments.

## Question
How serious is the impact of social media on distance learning courses? Judge for yourself. Suppose you are a professor teaching an online course and you receive the following e-mail from one of your students:

Hey prof, PLZ MIRL ASAP on assignment.

What would you do?

*Answer*
First, you may have to look up PLZ MIRL ASAP. In the texting and tweeting world, it means, "Please meet in real life as soon as possible." Then, you might realize that many students don't know how to write a professional e-mail. In the role of professor, we expect to see a greeting, a clearly articulated request, and a closing. Students must learn how to do that eventually. Should we should teach them those skills now? Can we do it in a distance learning and social media world?

## FLIPPED CLASSROOM

The dispute between advocates of in-person versus online courses might lead us to a solution that satisfies both camps. The flipped classroom is a type of blended learning that delivers instructional content outside of classroom. Lecture and "homework" switch places.

- **Course Content.** Students watch videos online while outside class. They include lectures and other prepared content that can require written reactions submitted to the professor.
- **Interactive Discussion.** The classroom is used to engage the concepts with the guidance of a mentor. No more taking notes or copying things from a blackboard. Time is spent thinking and talking by everyone, sometimes in small group discussions.

The flipped classroom allows teachers to identify materials, tools and support for learning while students set goals and manage their time. Replacing lectures increases in-class activity. Considerable evidence shows a higher level of learning.

## CONSIDER, IF YOU WILL, THE HYBRID COURSE

Hybrid courses, designed properly as flipped classrooms can work. To provide time for the "homework," classes meet less often by eliminating the time spent providing content via lectures. The professor and students spend their time together on critical thinking. They clarify concepts, exchange ideas, reflect upon contradictions, and otherwise engage. They modify the classic quote from Confucius:

> I hear and I forget. I see and I remember. I do and I understand.

What students do is "talk." Then, they remember.

**Question**
Can we measure student learning with online classes? How do we ensure that no one helps them with their multiple-choice exams?

*Answer*
Maybe you replace them with short-answer exercises where students use their own words. After all, exams are not restricted to fifty- or seventy-five-minute time limitations.

**Question**
What if students have a problem and need to talk to an instructor?

*Answer*
E-mail? Text? Telephone?

## QUIZ ON KNOWLEDGE OF ONLINE COURSES

Whatever else is happening in higher education, distance learning and hybrid courses are probably here to stay. Following is a quiz modeled on a U.S. News and World Report article. Answers follow.

Which of the following individuals earned an online MBA degree?

- Shaquille O'Neal.
- Taylor Swift.
- Tom Cruise.
- Lady Gaga.

How many U.S. students took an online course in 2016?

- 200 thousand.
- 2.5 million.
- 5.5 million.
- 12 million.

What online bachelor's program was ranked number one in the nation in 2016?

- Embry-Riddle Aeronautical University.
- Western Kentucky University.

- University of Southern California.
- Chicago State College.

Which of the following is the relationship of the cost of online and traditional college degree programs?

- Traditional almost always costs more.
- Traditional almost always costs less.
- They almost always cost about the same.
- None of the above.

What is the most popular field of study among online students?

- Psychology.
- Education.
- Business.
- Computer science.

Which of the following is not a common practice used to curb cheating in online courses?

- Keystroke recognition.
- Scanning user eyeball for ID confirmation.
- In-person proctored exam.
- Webcam proctored exam.

Which of the following occurs with an asynchronous online class?

- Students and instructors log in at the same time.
- Students and instructors log in at fixed scheduled time.
- Students log in at the same time as each other.
- Students log in whenever they want.

Which of the following is the meaning of MOOC?

- Massive Open Online Course.
- Modern Online Outsourced Course.
- Major Open Outsourced Course.
- Modern Outsourced Online Course

Which of the following is the least important for students who choose online courses?

- Faculty credentials.
- Cost.
- Reputation of the school.
- No specific times for class to meet.

Which of the following helps students to do better in an online course?

- Purchasing updated software.
- Taking an orientation session at the start of the course.
- Reviewing a textbook when viewing an online video.
- None of the above.

*Answers*

- Earned an online MBA degree. **Shaquille O'Neal.**
- Number of U.S. students who took an online course in 2016. **5.5 million.**
- Online bachelor's program ranked number one. **Embry-Riddle Aeronautical University.**
- Relationship of cost of online and traditional college degree programs. **Costs vary all over the place.**
- Most popular field among online students. **Business.**
- Not a common practice to curb cheating in online courses. **Scanning user eyeball for ID confirmation.**
- In an asynchronous online class. **Students log in whenever they want.**
- Meaning of MOOC. **Massive Open Online Course.**
- Least important for students of online courses. **Faculty credentials.**
- Helps students do better in online course. **Taking an orientation session at the start of the course.**

## Statistics for Online Classes

Whenever our view of online courses, many students take them. The data come from the National Center for Education Statistics (table 17.1).

Table 17.1  Percentage of Students Taking Online Courses

|  | Taking Online Courses (percent) | |
|---|---|---|
|  | At Least One | All Online |
| **Level of Enrollment** | | |
| Undergraduate | 73 | 11 |
| Graduate | 69 | 23 |
| **Category of Institution** | | |
| Public | 75 | 9 |
| Private nonprofit | 80 | 13 |
| Private for-profit | 41 | 52 |

## CONCLUSION

The landscape for hybrid and online courses is changing as colleges and universities try new methods of encouraging learning and new technology becomes available to them to do so. Rollins College faculty may be in the fortunate position of staying exclusively with a traditional format. Many other schools are taking advantage of new technology and formats for meeting the educational needs of their students.

*Chapter Eighteen*

# Does Academic Freedom Protect Anything That Needs Protecting? Would the Academy Collapse if Academic Freedom Went Away?

> The most important aspect of freedom of speech is freedom to learn ... That is the essence of academic freedom.
>
> —William O. Douglas, Supreme Court Justice

### BELIEVE IT OR NOT

Kenneth Howell, an adjunct associate professor, was teaching an introductory course on Catholicism at the University of Illinois. Prior to giving an exam, he sent an e-mail to his students explaining the church's belief that homosexual conduct is morally wrong. He framed the argument in the philosophical language of natural moral law.

A student complained to school officials that he was offended by the teaching. The university responded by informing Howell he would not teach the course next year. A group of Christian attorneys protested the action. The university quickly reversed its decision.

**Question**
Did the university acknowledge first amendment rights protecting the free exercise of speech?

*Answer*
No. The first amendment only applies to Congress passing laws against free speech. A concept called academic freedom prohibits censoring the professor's speech within the scope of the topic of the course. It even more pointedly bans efforts to quell speech that "offends."

# ACADEMIC FREEDOM

This term expresses a principle that freedom of inquiry by faculty members is essential to the mission of higher education. Professors should be able to research and communicate ideas or facts without fear of retaliation by college administrators. The protection covers activities that are inconvenient as well as those opposed by religious, political, or governmental authorities.

**Question**
A biology professor assigned students a study to protect wildlife near a local sewerage plant. One student wrote a paper critical of the mayor's actions. The student asked for permission to publish it in the student newspaper. Can the university block publication?

*Answer*
Supposedly not. Under academic freedom professors and students can engage in intellectual debate without fear of censorship or retaliation and can express their views in speech, writing, and electronic communication on and off campus without fear of sanction. This right does not apply to actions that violate the rights of others. Professors may not present views that show them to be ignorant, incompetent, or dishonest with respect to their field of expertise.

**Question**
A student posted a blog criticizing past actions of a scheduled graduation speaker. The University demanded that it be withdrawn. Does the student have to comply?

*Answer*
Not according to academic freedom. Faculty and students may study topics they choose, draw conclusions consistent with their research, and disseminate those views. They just cannot claim their ideas represent the views of the university.

**Question**
A university sponsors a study abroad program. It restricts participation to students who are registered Republicans. Is the university allowed to do this?

*Answer*
Not per academic freedom in the sense that political, religious, or philosophical beliefs cannot be imposed on students or faculty.

**Question**
A faculty member was awarded a university fellowship to study Hindu family practices. Subsequently, the academic vice president learned the professor was a practicing Moslem. He withdrew the approval stating a conflict of interest was present. Does he have the right to do this?

*Answer*
It depends upon the facts of the situation. Academic freedom affords some protection as the faculty member has the right to a hearing alleging his rights have been violated.

**Question**
A professor disagreed with a decision by the Board of Trustees and complained to a local newspaper. He was widely quoted complaining about one trustee. The board met and directed the president to punish the professor. What should the president do?

*Answer*
Nothing official. Academic freedom allows faculty members and students to publically disagree with administrative policies or proposals without fear of reprisal.

## UNIVERSITY RIGHTS

The U.S. Supreme Court ruled a college can "determine for itself on academic grounds who may teach, what may be taught, how it should be taught, and who may be admitted to study." Court rulings have generally protected academic freedom while restricting professor behaviors to that framework. Professors do not have any "freedom" to decide what may be taught, how it may be taught, and who may enroll in classes.

**Question**
A student repeatedly disagreed with a professor in class. The student obtained the grade of A on course assignments but received a final grade of C. When asked, the professor gave the student the grade of F for attendance and participation in class. The student appealed. What should the school do?

*Answer*
Investigate. Academic freedom allows faculty members and students to challenge each other's views but does not allow professors to penalize students for holding opposing views.

### Question
A university grievance committee sided with a student on a grade appeal. The dean demanded that the professor change the grade. The professor refused. Is the professor protected by academic freedom?

*Answer*
A federal court judge ruled that a professor has "no constitutional right to academic freedom ... that would prohibit senior (university) officials from changing a grade given by (a professor)." The professor cannot be coerced to change a grade. Instead, university officials may, in their discretionary authority, change the grade upon appeal by a student.

## RELATIONSHIP TO FREEDOM OF SPEECH

Many professors believe academic freedom and free speech rights are largely identical. Not quite. When professors speak or write in public, whether via social media or in academic journals, they need not fear institutional restriction or punishment when they avoid the appearance that they speak on behalf of the institution. Academic freedom is protected by institutional regulations, letters of appointment, faculty handbooks, collective bargaining agreements, and academic custom.

### Question
Two professors authored a paper accusing the board of trustees of criminal behavior by failing to ban the roundup and euthanizing of stray dogs and cats on the campus. One worked for a state university while the other worked for a private college. The presidents of both schools suspended the professors for one term without pay. Will a court uphold the suspension?

*Answer*
One may and one may not be upheld. Academic freedom has consistently been held to be a First Amendment right at public institutions. The reverse is true at private institutions where courts have given colleges options to restrict freedom of speech.

### Question
A student from Asia had difficulty with English and was graded down for poor writing on assigned papers. The student appealed the final grade. Is he likely to win the appeal?

*Answer*
The facts of the case will decide. Academic freedom gives faculty members the authority to assign grades as long as they are not capricious or unjustly punitive. The institution retains its right to maintain academic standards but must follow due process in disputes with faculty members.

**Question**
A psychology department has two factions. The majority of professors align with functionalism while the minority are humanists. The majority group approved a policy that all professors must use the same functionalism textbook for the introductory psychology course. One professor refused. The department requested enforcement of its vote. What should the university do?

*Answer*
Academic freedom offers faculty members substantial latitude in deciding how to teach the courses for which they are responsible. The university should set up a hearing to decide how to resolve the dispute.

**Question**
An athlete is being investigated by the police on a serious misbehavior charge. His coach may have helped the individual to misbehave. The faculty senate requested suspension of the coach. What should the president do?

*Answer*
Academic freedom guarantees that serious charges against a faculty member will be heard before a committee of his or her peers. The president should establish an independent hearing and due process including the right for the coach to bring in an attorney.

## PUBLIC SPEECH AND ACADEMIC FREEDOM

Ivor van Heerden, PhD, was a professor at Louisiana State University (LSU) when he wrote a book critical of the U.S. Army Corps of Engineers efforts to protect New Orleans in advance of Hurricane Katrina in 2005.

He was vocal in the media with his criticism. LSU, fearing the loss of federal grant monies, requested that he cease his public statements. He declined to do so.

In April 2009, LSU fired him. He said publicly, "I learned about [it] through the news media. They basically didn't have the guts to tell me that to my face ..."

**Question**
Dr. van Heerden alleged a violation of academic freedom. The AAUP sided with him. He sued LSU. What happened?

*Answer*
LSU eventually settled the case by paying the professor $435,000, after spending more than $600,000 for legal fees. van Heerden left higher education and became a writer and documentary producer to educate the public on environmental issues.

## COURSE GRADES AND ACADEMIC FREEDOM

Another LSU story involves Dominique Homberger, a tenured full professor, who was repeatedly commended for teaching excellence in her "rigorous approach" and "demanding coursework for biology majors." In 2010, she was assigned to teach an introductory course for the first time in fifteen years. Her mid-term grades were strongly skewed to Ds and Fs.

The dean, without consulting her, replaced her as the instructor in the course. She filed a complaint with LSU's Faculty Grievance Committee and the AAUP. Both bodies found LSU violated her academic freedom by suspending her without academic due process.

**Question**
Dr. Homberger gave brief quizzes at the beginning of every class. She did not curve exams. Her multiple-choice questions had ten possible answers. Do you agree with the LSU decision to remove her from introductory biology?

*Answer*
No. The university should conduct a hearing. Academic freedom allows two viewpoints to be expressed within the constraints of due process.

Whatever your view, academic freedom considers:

- **Goals of Instructor Behavior.** A quiz at the start of each class encourages reading materials in advance and attending every class. Avoiding a curve can have a goal of achieving mastery of subject matter rather than simply doing better than weaker students. Ten multiple-choice answers reduce the success of guessing.
- **Responsibility of University Administrators.** The institution has the right to select for admission students that can graduate. Excessive expectations on student capabilities by an instructor is a student rights and responsibilities issue.

## CONTROVERSIAL MESSAGES AND ACADEMIC FREEDOM

Professor S. Jay Olshansky regularly and publically criticized the American Academy of Anti-Aging Medicine as presenting false evidence on how to reverse the aging process. The organization sued the University of Illinois professor accusing him of intentional defamation.

UIC, not a defendant in the suit, paid the professor's legal bills explaining, "It's the job of a university professor to search for the truth and to speak it. The professor was doing his job."

The antiaging academy disagreed. "The statements were made outside the classroom and far removed from any claimed 'professional' conduct."

**Question**
Does the plaintiff have a valid claim for damages from the professor?

*Answer*
Maybe yes, maybe no. Academic freedom does not protect a professor from legal liability. We have no answer in this case as both sides settled with what one party called "a modest flow of capital in the general direction of lawyers."

## CAMPUS ATTITUDES ON FREEDOM OF SPEECH

The Chronicle of Higher Education sampled faculty views on the exchange of ideas on U.S. campuses in 2016. Some quotes, slightly edited:

> Without question, campus environments have become much more free. The real problem is that they don't like the free speech they are hearing.

> We are living in the greatest era of freely available speech in the history of higher education. Network technologies have broadened the scope of public discourse on and around campus.

> Overall, considerably more free. The much greater diversity among students provides a wider range of perspectives.

> It's cyclical. Waves of political correctness hit campuses in the late 1960s, 1970s, and late 1980s. Now we're seeing another such wave. In any case, the Internet has been a boon for all forms of dissent.

The exchange of ideas has become both more and less free. More, in the sense that communications technologies enable dialogue that would have been unimaginable 50 years ago. Less, as with walls between factions that make it harder to truly listen.

## CONCLUSION

Academic freedom is a fundamental concept in higher education. It is elaborately structured, fiercely supported, and widely misunderstood. On balance, it probably protects faculty, administration, and trustees from temptation to misbehave in disputes on ideology, research, and teaching.

*Chapter Nineteen*

# Does Tenure Protect Anything That Needs Protecting? Would the Academy Collapse if Tenure Went Away?

Can a geology teacher blithely tell his students that the earth is flat? That's not academic freedom, but dereliction of duty.

—Jerry A. Coyne, professor

### BELIEVE IT OR NOT

A professor was teaching two courses. One was Principles of Economics. The other was Principles of Insurance. He gave both classes the same mid-term exam, a repeat of an insurance class exam given three years earlier. Students complained to the dean. What happened?

*Answer*
Nothing. The professor had tenure. All the students got grades of B or better. The matter was dropped.

**Question**
A professor started the term with four courses, nineteen to twenty-three students in each. After the first class period when students could change courses without financial penalties, the enrollment dropped to seven to thirteen students. What happened?

*Answer*
Nothing. The professor had tenure.

## Question

A professor taught four courses a semester on Tuesdays and Thursday at 8:00 am, 9:30 am. 11:00 am, and 2:00 pm. He did not take attendance and gave a two-hour final exam that counted for 100 percent of the grade. He had office hours on Tuesday from 1:30 to 2:00 pm. He never came to campus on nonteaching days and advised few students. The only college function he attended was graduation. He worked thirty hours a week as a counselor in a medical clinic near the campus. Several students complained to the dean. What happened?

*Answer*
Nothing. The professor had tenure.

## Question

A professor taught an online class. Students purchased a textbook, completed the exercises in the back of it, and e-mailed them to the professor. He did not respond to them. On the last day of the term, he posted the grades without explanation on the students' Blackboard accounts. Several parents complained to the academic vice president. What happened?

*Answer*
Nothing. The professor had tenure.

In these cases, college officials discussed the situation with the professors. The professors defended their behavior. No administrator deemed it viable to take any corrective action.

## WHAT IS TENURE?

Tenure in higher education is the right to keep a job for as long as you want. An alternative definition is it is a status granted after a trial period to protect a college teacher from dismissal without a formal hearing process. Both definitions are correct but they are not always accurate. The meaning of tenure depends on who you ask.

### Justification for Tenure

The American Association of University Professors (AAUP) is the leading advocate for protecting tenure. Without it, academic freedom is weakened as faculty members are less likely to take risks in the classroom or in their scholarship. The free exchange of ideas may be hampered by the fear of dismissal.

Most independent research does not fully support these viewpoints. Tenure may not be the only way to protect the integrity of the academy.

## History of Tenure

We can trace tenure back to the mid-1800s when professors largely served at the pleasure of the president, academic dean, or board of trustees. The system began to change at Cornell in the 1870s, the University of Wisconsin in 1894, and other universities after that. By 1910, many colleges observed de facto tenure. Other than offenses involving religious principles, colleges did not attempt to discipline professors for divergent views.

In 1915, the AAUP published a declaration of principles for academic freedom and tenure. Its premises were as follows:

- Only committees of faculty members are qualified to judge a member of the faculty.
- Faculty appointments should be made by other faculty and chairpersons accompanied by contracts with explicit grounds for dismissal.

In 1940, the AAUP added that the probationary period for tenure would be a maximum of seven years and a tenured professor cannot be dismissed without adequate cause and justification after due process.

The 1970s started a steady decline in the percentage of tenure-track and tenured college and university teaching positions. If tenure was the holy grail, it became increasingly hard to get. Today's situation with contingency faculty reflects the decline.

## Question
A professor failed to file a request for tenure in the sixth year and started the seventh year without notice of termination. When the vice president discovered the omission, he told the chair to send a registered letter to the professor that he was in his final year. The chair refused. What happened?

*Answer*
The university legal counsel was consulted. The university faculty handbook required one year's notice before the end of a tenure-track appointment. The deadline was missed. The faculty member was entitled to start year eight and thus had de facto tenure.

## DISMISSAL FOR CAUSE

When termination is based upon performance, a school must show cause in a formal hearing process. Examples are insubordination, incompetence, neglect of duty, substantial noncompliance with school policies, immoral conduct, and conviction of a crime.

## Due Process

The effort to remove tenure must follow due process. A college or university is expected to identify the procedural requirements, give written notice of dismissal along with the reason for it, and allow a fair and meaningful hearing that will, in most cases, include participation by other tenured professors.

## Financial Exigency

Separately from revoking tenure for cause, an institution may declare financial exigency as a justification. An example is a severe financial crisis affecting the institution or its academic integrity.

## Discontinuance for Educational Reasons

AAUP also recognizes that tenure can be revoked because of a legitimate formal discontinuance of a program or department of instruction. The decision must reflect long-range judgments with respect to the educational mission of the institution.

# WISCONSIN'S 2016 TENURE POLICY CHANGE

In 2016, Wisconsin changed the tenure policy for state colleges and universities. Specifically, a tenured professor could be dismissed if a school closed, curtailed, or modified an academic program or department. The change reduced the faculty role in making such a decision.

The action enraged senior professors who argued the action destroyed tenure, severely weakened shared faculty governance, and basically meant the board of regents could "fire anyone, at any time, for any reason."

## Question

One faculty member used Twitter to advise incoming freshmen, "We don't want students 2 waste their $" and "We are all leaving. No joke." Was she right about professors leaving?

*Answer*

Somewhat. She and five other high-profile tenured faculty members were "poached" by other universities. Forty who had offers eventually stayed, mostly because Wisconsin increased their salaries and research support.

**Question**
Does Wisconsin's new policy violate AAUP guidelines?

*Answer*
Apparently not. The AAUP expressed a concern and pointed out that such an effort can be an attempt to conceal violations of academic freedom and tenure.

**Question**
Will Wisconsin experience problems recruiting new superstars because the university cannot promise them "proper tenure?"

*Answer*
Yes, per some faculty members.

**Question**
Does the new policy limit faculty research to the "whims of eighteen people appointed by a governor (board of regents) with an antieducation agenda?"

*Answer*
That's the view of at least one faculty member.

**Question**
The new policy is not likely to affect the vast majority of Wisconsin professors. Why are they so upset?

*Answer*
One professor explained that professors are not egotistic. They do not think they are better or smarter than others. They want tenure "to protect the integrity of the knowledge they produce and disseminate" at the university. We can wonder whether this is true.

**Question**
Does university research matter?

*Answer*
Yes, per opponents of Wisconsin's new policy. Universities deserve credit for technological and social advances in urban planning, alleviating poverty and hunger, eradicating diseases, and improving infrastructure. Without tenure, corporate greed and power would endanger research.

**Question**
With respect to the university and disgruntled faculty, who's right?

*Answer*
A question to be answered by each professor.

## IS TENURE A LITMUS TEST?

This is an odd question. A litmus test was discovered in medieval universities in the fourteenth century. If a substance is acid, litmus paper turns red. It turns blue in alkaline solutions.

Today, we use the term "litmus test" figuratively to identify any single factor that establishes the true character of someone or something. It applies to political, moral, or ethical opinions.

Tenure is a litmus test of sorts. It may be awarded or denied based upon a single factor. Colleges will openly tell tenure-track professors that a litmus test exists for tenure. Tenured colleagues who vote on tenure will not explain a positive or negative vote. What about hidden litmus tests?

- One refereed journal article per year while on the tenure track.
- One tenured faculty member on the Rank and Tenure Committee who hates something you said in a department meeting.
- One senior administrator who believes no one of your religious persuasion should receive a permanent appointment.
- Three liberal members of a department who do not want to give the conservative coalition another colleague.

### Question

A candidate interviewed for a position in the finance department at a major state university. He asked what the standards were for tenure. He was told that five publications in five years were required in one of the following journals:

- *Quarterly Journal of Economics*
- *Econometrica*
- *Journal of Financial Economics*
- *Journal of Economic Literature*
- *Review of Economic Studies*
- *American Economic Journal: Applied Economics*
- *American Economic Review*

What did he do?

### Answer

He withdrew his application. When asked why, he said, "I want to publish in journals that somebody reads."

Aside from publication in a restricted area, the stumbling blocks of a litmus test are everywhere. They are not marked by "Beware—Road to Tenure Wiped Out." Who did you offend when the following happened?

- You participated in the faculty union. Or refused to participate.
- You expressed your attitude about gun control, gay rights, or illegal immigrants.
- You openly and honestly discussed a controversial issue in the classroom.
- You supported the inclusion of courses in the core curriculum. Or their removal.
- You failed to "curve" your grades. Or curved them.

**Question**
Students aspiring to become licensed clinical psychologists choose one of two types of doctorates. Both programs take five to seven years to complete. One is a doctor of psychology, PsyD. The other a doctor of philosophy, PhD. A newly minted assistant professor chose the PsyD because she wanted to do research involving patients in therapy. Is the choice of the degree a litmus test?

*Answer*
Absolutely, in many environments. Psychologists may know the difference but members of the P&T committee often have a bias that only a PhD meets the grade. She may subsequently learn that her degree choice cannot be offset by other criteria.

## IS BEING A REPUBLICAN A LITMUS TEST?

Perhaps we missed an important litmus test in the academy. Don't concepts such as academic freedom and tenure protect all professors? What about Republicans?

**Question**
If a professor is a Democrat, does that mean he is a liberal? If she is a Republican, is she a conservative?

*Answer*
Professors seem to think so and evidence generally seems to support them.

The 2016 presidential race focused on a divide between liberals and conservatives. Many people assume the great bulk of Republicans are conservative while Democrats are liberals. Going from this premise, the 2016 popular vote in the presidential election race contains some interesting data. It confirms somewhat the isolation of Republicans, and by extension conservatives, on the campus.

A *Chronicle of Higher Education* article right after the election was titled, "Yes, You're Right, Colleges Are Liberal Bubbles." It argues that about 80 percent of professors at public state flagship universities are Democratic and "liberal." Maybe not in Utah and Mississippi but nationwide.

## Question
As the popular vote across the whole country split almost evenly between Trump and Clinton, how can researchers claim colleges are liberal bubbles?

*Answer*
They compared voting districts with flagship state universities to the results of the entire state for forty-nine states. Districts with major universities gave 60 percent of their votes to Clinton. Examples:

- **University of North Carolina.** Clinton got 74 percent in Orange County and 47 percent statewide.
- **University of Maryland.** Clinton got 89 percent in Prince George's County and 60 percent statewide.
- **Universities in "Trump Strongholds.** Clinton did not do well in Oklahoma, West Virginia, and similar 'red' states," but she did better in all the university counties than she did statewide.

The results of the 2016 presidential election may have serious long-term repercussions in the academy. Democrats were terrified after the election. Predictions of a widespread apocalypse included ideology and economics. Headlines and story summaries are given below:

- **Mike Pence Wants Creationism Taught in Public Schools.** Pence argues that evolution is "only a theory" and that public schools should teach intelligent design as well as evolution. According to him, only intelligent design provides a "rational explanation for the known universe."
- **Trump and the Fall of Liberalism.** After the electoral explosion, liberals fear years in the wilderness. The Democrats' exile "is likely to be lengthy."
- **How Did Trump Get Elected?** This piece argues that Trump's victory is consistent with a global trend in favor of authoritarian national populism over the inefficiencies and corruptions of liberal democracy.

**Question**
Given the tensions of the 2016 presidential race, we ask, "Does tenure protect Republican professors from their Democratic colleagues?"

*Answer*
Time will tell but first they must get it if "republicanism" is a litmus test with liberal professors.

## CONCLUSION

The debate about the protections offered by tenure are likely to continue for some time. One group believes it protects academic freedom and hard-working and committed faculty. It may offer a safe harbor to incompetent or lazy professors. We do not resolve any issues here. The trend toward contingency faculty, as already discussed, may be a sign of what is happening aside from the debates.

*Part V*

# CAREER DECISION-MAKING FOR PROFESSORS

*Chapter Twenty*

# Despite It All, Would You Like to Be a Professor? Can You Tell Me More about Academic Purgatory?

> Now Purgatory, the second kingdom where the soul of man is cleansed, made worthy to ascend to Heaven.
>
> —Dante Alighieri

### THE TEMPTATION OF PROFESSORSHIP

Pursuing the life of a professor can be tempting. To pursue it, you should answer some questions.

- What should I do with my degree or past experience? Is it enough to pave the way to a college or university?
- What do I need to do and when do I need to do it? I have a master's degree. Is that enough? I want to teach but what kind of research might be interesting?
- What kind of obstacles will I face? Will I be able to finish the right degree or publish in the right places?

Most of us have obsessions of one kind or another. We need to understand what we want, who we are, and what works for us. A great student does not always make a good professor. If a person never did much writing, scholarly recognition may not be on the table. If you dislike working with undergraduates, what are we talking about?

One reality is that a specific college or university determines what it wants. You just fit the bill. Answer two questions: Am I a teacher, scholar, or administrator? Which one does the school want? Things are not likely to work out so well for a classroom teacher who accepts a position where research is the primary expectation.

**Question**
How can we find out what a college or university is really looking for in a recruiting ad?

*Answer*
Look for the clues.

- The school wants a teacher if the scholarship statement is weak. "Scholarship and service to the university are also expected."
- The school is seeking publication if the announced goal is enhanced reputation. "We are proud to be one of the top schools in the region."

Few professors are both good teachers and scholars. If you are neither, a faculty position is clearly the wrong goal to pursue.

## AT THE FOOT OF MOUNT PURGATORY

In Dante's *The Divine Comedy*, the Mountain of Purgatory is on an island on the far side of the world. Its terraces correspond to the seven deadly sins, all of which arise from two types of love:

- **Perverted Love.** The sins of biblical pride (arrogance), greed, and lust that cause harm to others.
- **Deficient Love.** Envy, gluttony, wrath, and sloth representing excessive love of good things.

At some point, you may find yourself torn between worldly opportunities and a permanent position in the academy. Weigh your goals against your perilous climb. This is time for a little introspection.

## HIDDEN TRAPS

The decision to pursue the academy should make you consider the "hidden traps" that distort decision-making. A 2009 article in the *Harvard Business Review* can help identify obsessions.

## Bandwagon Effect

This occurs when we believe something because others believe it. "Everybody says accounting is a worthwhile career field. Thus, I trained to be an accountant when I was in college."

### Question
An assistant professor at a private liberal arts college is in the second year of a tenure-track appointment. She has one scholarly publication and good student evaluations. Her tenured colleagues pointed out the many advantages of teaching in public state universities. Following their encouragement, she resigned and took an assistant professor post at one such university. How did it work out?

*Answer*
Not well. The advice of her colleagues blinded her to her own love of teaching small classes. Almost immediately, she was uncomfortable in tiered lecture halls. The stress caused a decline in her scholarly activity with predictable impact. She did not get tenure and promotion. The bandwagon effect at work?

## Confirmation Bias

This is a tendency to search for or interpret information to confirm one's preconceptions. "I once knew a lawyer and did not like him. Thus, I do not want to consider the law as a career field."

### Question
An associate professor slowed down his research after achieving tenure. He began to suspect that editors of journals accepted the work of their own disciples. In other cases, he claimed "one hand washes the other," meaning editors accepted each other's submissions. He discussed with his colleagues the rejection of his submissions to scholarly journals. What did he hope to learn?

*Answer*
Maybe nothing. He may be searching for confirmation that the system was rigged.

## Endowment Effect

This occurs when people demand more to give up an object than they would pay to acquire it. "I have a good job. Why would I make a change?"

**Question**
A tenured associate professor asked another professor about working together on a joint research project. Both taught at major public universities. The associate professor did two-thirds of the work and asked to be first author on the publication. The professor balked saying, "I am higher rank and my school is more prestigious." What is happening here?

*Answer*
Maybe the endowment effect? "I am a full professor. You are not. What I bring to the table is more valuable than what you bring to it."

## IRRATIONAL ESCALATION

This is the tendency to make irrational decisions based upon decisions in the past. It also is used to justify actions already taken. "What else could I do? My strategy worked in my prior college. I could do nothing else."

**Question**
A lecturer was well liked by students. His colleagues told him he was indispensable as the only instructor who could teach a required course. The department chair told him to adopt a specific textbook for the course. He refused and threatened to quit. The chair backed off. Three years later the dean told him the same thing. Once again he refused. What happened?

*Answer*
The dean accepted his resignation. Is this irrational escalation?

### Déformation Professionnelle

This is a psychological term implying that professional training can distort decision-making. The concept is captured in the phrase, "When the only tool you have is a hammer, every problem looks like a nail." "I am trained in economics. This is a position that is not suited to an economist. I will not pursue it."

**Question**
A professor taught an advanced course in a large lecture hall for many years. His lectures were well received by students. A new dean converted the course to a seminar and restricted enrollment to twenty students per section. The professor did not change his lectures. How did she do?

*Answer*
Her student evaluations plunged. Was it déformation professionnelle?

## Status Quo Trap

Once committed to a job, people are reluctant to change. Something buried deep within our subconscious immobilizes us even when we know we will never get tenure or promotion. An opportunity comes along and we decline it. We rationalize the situation. We fear the risk of making a change.

### Question
An assistant professor has a five-year renewable contract with a university. In the second year, she receives an offer for a tenure-track position at a college with a lower reputation for scholarship. Should she change jobs?

*Answer*
Whatever the answer, she may have to overcome the fear of making a change.

## Sunk Cost Trap

A sunk cost is money or energy already spent and permanently lost. It cannot be recovered. The sunk cost trap occurs when a decision is made relative to a past action that has no bearing on the present or future. "I bought an oil company stock five years ago and made money. I will buy another one today."

### Question
Three years ago, an individual joined a faculty and now earns a salary of $80,000. A better offer came along except another college could only offer $75,000. He declined the interview explaining, "I cannot go back. I need at least $82,000." Is this a good strategy?

*Answer*
The fact that he earned a higher salary previously has no bearing on the decision. Either the job makes sense or it does not.

## Anchoring Trap

This occurs when a person locks in on a statement with a clear positive or negative reference point. "Even though a school offers a high salary and excellent teaching situation, faculty offices are small. Therefore, the job is not acceptable."

### Question
A doctoral candidate is discussing the acceptance of an assistant professor, tenure-track position with a private college. Early in the interviewing process, she is asked about the salary she seeks. Her answer is $65,000.

She does not know that the college has set a salary range from $60,000 to $80,000 for the position. Is she in good shape with the response?

*Answer*
The statement immediately establishes a framework for the remaining discussion. The college does not have to pay more than $65,000 and might offer less. An applicant must be ready for the question but it may not be wise to anchor the salary too early in the negotiation.

## LAUNCHING THE JOURNEY

As we reflect upon the steep climb up Mount Purgatory, all the "facts" may not line up. We may just have to "feel" a course of action. Other times, a "gut feel" is not enough. We want details and time to analyze options. Well, we just need to decide whether to go for it.

Again we turn to Malcolm Gladwell and two approaches to making decisions.

- **Thick Slice.** Uses available information to ensure a comprehensive evaluation of all the factors.
- **Thin Slice.** Uses a quick assessment of what seems to be relevant factors followed by a speedy decision.

Professors generally do not like thin slicing. They characterize it as "seat of the pants" or "quick and dirty." Gladwell is an advocate of thin slicing. Too much information allows irrelevant factors to affect our judgment. If you want to teach, find a school that wants teachers. If you want to write, find one that values publication. If you want money, look away from the professoriate.

Considerable research in psychology and philosophy shows that thin slicing can be as accurate, oftentimes more accurate, than judgments based on much more information.

### The Thin Slice of Bias

Professors have a bias for colleagues they want. If we think about it, everybody has that problem. "We only hire professors from the top schools." "We reserve tenure for a small portion of candidates." "We only accept scholarship published in a few journals."

Bias is a thin slice. We ignore it at our peril.

## Question

The members of a department discussed recruiting a new assistant professor. They agreed that the ability to teach principles of economics was the biggest need. Two comments were made:

> **Professor "A":** We need someone who has experience with how governments shape monetary and fiscal policy.
>
> **Professor "B":** We need someone who understands capitalism, relative pricing, and the allocation of limited resources.

Who is right?

*Answer*

Maybe neither. How about overlooking the bias of course content and looking for someone who can explain all topics in an introductory course?

## Bias among Professionals

Decision-making bias is not limited to professors in the academy. It is visible among doctors, lawyers, artists, musicians, and most other professionals. We cannot get rid of it. We need to manage it.

## Question

Orchestra leaders watched individuals play an instrument and then evaluated the quality of the performance. Most auditions had the same outcome. Men were better musicians and thus dominated orchestras. Musician unions claimed a bias against females and demanded a different format. They sought a formal committee to replace the conductor and demanded screens so committee members could not see the musician. If a musician gave any sign of their gender, the individual would leave the hall and be assigned a new number. Did anything change?

*Answer*

Malcolm Gladwell gave this as an example of bias of professionals. Orchestra leaders once held auditions for new members in hotel rooms or auditoriums. The result when auditions became anonymous was that women became an important component of U.S. orchestras.

## Question

Is the same kind of bias in force when professors add newcomers to their own ranks?

*Answer*

Not exactly. It is probably safe to assume that most orchestra leaders want to add the best possible musicians to the ensemble. Professors are often motivated to avoid adding scholars or teachers who outshine them with research or in the classroom.

## Freud on Thin Slices

People may not even know they have subconscious bias. It is not a new concept. We can trace it back to Sigmund Freud (1856–1939):

> *When making a decision of minor importance, I have always found it advantageous to consider all the pros and cons. In vital matters, however, such as the choice of a mate or a profession, the decision should come from the unconscious, from somewhere inside ourselves.*

We should remember the advice of Freud and Gladwell about thin slice decisions. Anybody with experience in faculty meetings knows that prolonged discussion does not usually improve decision-making.

## CONCLUSION

OK. We're going to do it. If you got this far, you are either in purgatory, passed through it, or want to start the journey leading to it. Let's create the thin slice picture.

- Get a doctorate.
- Write a dissertation.
- Choose the school wisely.
- Get tenure.

*Chapter Twenty-one*

# Can You Believe Limbo Is the Next Stop after Purgatory? Where, Oh Where, Is Tenure?

The more a thing is perfect, the more it feels pleasure and pain.

—Dante Alighieri

### BELIEVE IT OR NOT

If we want success in the academy, we should try to produce an unstoppable change. Create circumstances that excite the emotions. Achieve a status that has a major impact. Malcolm Gladwell coined the term "tipping point" to describe such a moment.

**Question**
Some professors identified the biggest "tipping point" in the academy.

**Professor "C."** A Pulitzer Prize for excellence in writing.
**Professor "D."** A Nobel Prize for lifetime achievement.
**Professor "E."** Presidential recognition at the Kennedy Center Honors.
**Professor "F."** A MacArthur Fellows "Genius Grant."

Who is right?

*Answer*
These are all prestigious and impressive but any chance for them occurs a long time after achieving success. Most academics pursue two tipping points.

- **First.** Successfully completing a dissertation.
- **Second.** Achieving tenure.

## COMPLETING THE DISSERTATION

The dissertation is the last terrace on Mount Purgatory. It is reminiscent of the final torment through which all sinners must pass to leave purgatory:

> [T]he last and most terrifying trial is a wall of flame before which Dante stops short in terror. When he plunges in, he feels as though bathing in molten glass would be a relief from the pain ... The same trial awaits everyone.

Compare this to a description of the dissertation approval process:

> [T]he last and most terrifying trial is a creation of a maddening and totally obtuse research project, before which the candidate cringes in pain and terror. When he or she plunges in, it as though bathing in molten glass would be a relief from the pain ... The same trial awaits every future doctorally qualified professor.

The trials of the dissertation will not be covered here. They are covered in detail in my book *Culture, Intricacies, and Obsessions in Academia: Why Colleges and Universities are Struggling to Deliver the Goods*, where three chapters are titled as follows:

- What Is the Conundrum of the Doctoral Dissertation?
- Is It Worth All the Grief to Complete a Doctoral Dissertation?
- Would Anyone Respect a Tripartite Dissertation?

## A MISPLACED LIMBO

In *The Divine Comedy*, limbo is a region on the edge of hell for those who are not saved even though they did not sin. It is technically the first circle of hell but living conditions are not that bad. It's a reasonably comfortable place that includes virtuous non-Christian adults and unbaptized infants. They have no chance to go to heaven but they can hang around forever with little pleasure or pain.

In the academy, we see that limbo has been moved. It is not a circle of hell before you reach purgatory. You arrive in limbo after the dissertation. It holds those poor souls who are not baptized or, in the jargon of higher education, those who do not have tenure.

**Question**
Achieving a tenure-track position marks those waiting for baptism in sight of *The Earthly Paradise*. For Dante, heaven was divided into the spheres of fortitude, justice, temperance, prudence, faith, hope, and love. What are the spheres that can be seen from outside the gates by the tenure-track professor?

*Answer*
Maybe academic freedom, a lifelong appointment, plenty of time to write and reflect, lighter teaching loads, and travel money to attend professional conferences.

**Question**
But wait. The tenure track offers relative comfort as compared to the academic purgatory. Why do you need tenure to truly be inside the Earthly Paradise?

*Answer*
An easy answer. Without tenure, you can be expelled from paradise. Plus, you have no pressure if you do not want it. The status of tenured professors in the academy is something like angels in Dante's paradise.

## PURSUIT OF TENURE

Once you receive a tenure-track appointment, you must teach and publish a bit. Some suggestions in addition to those already shared. Maintain a low profile so no jealous colleague notices you. Try to find one or more powerful senior faculty friends who will protect and take care of you. Then, you are in the right place to wait for tenure. Just hope it is also the right time.

**Question**
Universities believe they grant tenure to the "best and the brightest" of their academic "stars." Is this true?

*Answer*
Not likely, at least based on anecdotal observations. We all had college instructors. Were they all stars?

## PEER REVIEW IS THE PATH OUT OF LIMBO

You can increase the odds to get tenure if you publish in obscure peer-reviewed journals. Comply with the madness.

Start with Wikipedia's sixty-three separate listings of journals by topical area. Move on to Ulrich's list to get a verification the publication is peer-reviewed or has equivalent editorial control of quality. Check out the SENSE publishing categories with rankings as refereed, other academic, and nonacademic publications. A recent list contains the following:

| Category | Number of Publishers |
| --- | --- |
| A. Top Publishers | 10 |
| B. Semi-top Publishers | 73 |
| C. Other Refereed Publishers | 188 |
| D. For an Academic Audience | 341 |
| E. For a General Audience | 158 |
| **All Publications** | **770** |

## PUBLISHING YOUR DISSERTATION

This is a contrary suggestion for newly minted PhDs and equivalent:

**Do not attempt to publish your dissertation!**

As previously stated, nobody cares about it. Ignore the advice of your mentor and new colleagues. Maybe you can use it to create articles. Some steps:

- **Findings.** Identify five findings in the dissertation.
- **Literature.** Write three to five pages as background for the first finding. Focus on including results from contemporary and respected researchers.
- **Primary Research.** Explain what you did to achieve the finding.
- **Significance.** Explain why your finding is important. If it is not important, pretend it is.
- **Further Research.** Explain where researchers can go next to build upon your finding.
- **Abstract and Conclusion.** Put in a starting and ending paragraph.
- **Repetition.** Repeat the process four more times for the other findings.

Select five journals and send one article to each one. If it is rejected, send it to another journal. If revisions are requested, make them. Keep up the process until you have at least three acceptances.

With mediocre teaching and occasional service, that should do it for promotion to associate professor with tenure if you also observe campus politics.

## THE POLITICS OF TENURE

Probationary faculty members are encouraged to cultivate colleagues across the campus. Who do you know? How can they help you? Remember our earlier discussion on connections. Strong connections exist with the members of our department and colleagues on committees where we serve. Weak connections are interactions with professors, administrators, fellow students, and other casual acquaintances in the academic setting. Promote relationships with both categories of people.

**Question**
An assistant professor knew she was coming up for tenure review next year. She asked her colleague if he would be willing to serve on P&T committee. Did he serve?

*Answer*
Sort of. He was elected to a three-year term, served one year during which his colleague received promotion and tenure, and then resigned. In P&T committee meetings, he reportedly was a strong advocate in favor of his departmental colleague.

**Question**
A campus has a specific requirement for scholarly publication as a prerequisite for promotion to the rank of associate professor. It also does not award tenure without the promotion. A popular tenure-track assistant professor came up before the P&T committee. He had little scholarship activity. Did he get the promotion and tenure?

*Answer*
Yes. He had three strong advocates on the P&T committee as a result of working with them on other college committees. They fought for him. The compromise was tenure without promotion. The dean accepted the recommendation.

The trick to overcoming the P&T committee hurdle is partly politics and partly understanding the weak connections on the committee.

**Question**
The faculty members in the department of education value working with students on their internships with local school districts. Scholarly publication and presentations are not stressed. A faculty member exhibits high energy and is successful helping students become certified as teachers. Is this a good sign for tenure prospects?

*Answer*
Partly. It should produce a strong recommendation from the department chair and colleagues. It still would be wise to cultivate faculty in other departments to ensure they agree with the balance of teaching and scholarship.

## BACKUP PLAN FOR TENURE

It's the first year on the tenure track. You are teaching courses with twenty-five or more students in each one. A barrage of additional trivial duties. You made it. Summer finally arrived. Now you can rest. Or can you?

There is no rest for the weary on the tenure track. There is only the task of managing time. Nobody on the search committee told you about two critical tasks that must be done.

- **Scholarship.** Oh sure, it says tenure is awarded based upon teaching, scholarship, and service. No problem, there. You have tons of good stories on two of these things. Doesn't everyone realize there is no time to write? Don't count on it.
- **External Connections.** You are now part of the academy, an extensive venture with more than a million fellow travelers. You don't know many of them. Is this a mistake? Yes, if you do not get tenure.

## CONCLUSION

Therefore, we conclude our introduction to the limbo of the postdissertation years prior to entry into the heavenly status of tenure. Only one more stop on the road. What are our choices after purgatory but before limbo and tenure?

*Chapter Twenty-two*

# Do You Know You Can Choose Your Own Limbo or Paradise?

## *Does God Give Us so Many Options Simply Because She Loves Us?*

> We are the ones we've been waiting for. We are the change that we seek.
> —Barack Obama

Dante had purgatory divided into terraces. In the modern academy, it consists of eleven isolated islands with occasional voyages to visit penitents on other islands. They are described in Colin Woodard's books *American Nations* and *American Character*.

### EPIC STRUGGLES IN NORTH AMERICA

Woodard argues that the United States and Canada have been engaged in an "epic struggle" since the late eighteenth century. Two forces are at play:

- **Individual Liberty.** The freedom from external restraint by the government in the exercise of personal rights. The focal points are freedom to move about, equality under the law, security of private property, and freedom of conscience and expression.
- **Common Good.** The benefits shared by members of a community. Focal points are improvements in health and welfare and active participation in politics and public service.

Similarly, the academy has been engaged in a struggle between among two forces:

- **Academic Freedom.** By this point we know well the efforts to protect freedom of inquiry and the communication of ideas without fear of retaliation.

- **Common Good.** The benefits for faculty and students in the process of acquiring and sharing knowledge.

Tensions exist and occasionally flare up in conflicts among the unmitigated rights of professors, the welfare of students, and efforts by the board and administration to manage the institution. We can see them in the classroom, in the faculty lounge, during office hours, on research projects, and in community events.

## MULTIPLE LEVELS OF PURGATORY

Although we refer to the academy as an all-encompassing entity, nothing could be further from the truth. We can divide, classify, and stratify higher education into public, private, profit, and nonprofit. Two-year, four-year, master's, and comprehensive. Teaching or research. Doctorate-granting, master's, baccalaureate, associates, special focus, and tribal.

Mount Purgatory had seven levels of deadly sins. An aspiring professor will find two levels in the academic version.

- **Entry Level.** This is a designation of a college or university as per the degrees it offers.
- **Pursuit of Permanent Appointment.** This is the probationary period leading up to tenure or three- to five-year (somewhat) automatic renewals.

Sage advice to shorten the time in purgatory is to choose wisely. If you want to do research and do not want to teach, stay away from community colleges. If you hate the pressure of publishing, stay away from "publish or perish" institutions.

## ELEVEN ACADEMIC PURGATORIES

Unlike Dante's world, purgatory is not a single fixed designation. Any of the 4,500 U.S. and Canadian institutions can serve as a refuge for sinners seeking redemption. A professor can choose from eleven discreet regions identified by Colin Woodard. Their values are shaped by the struggle between individual liberty and the common good. Each region creates its own purgatory.

### 1. Yankeedom

Roughly New York and New England, with a capital city of Boston, professors seek to create a perfect society pursuing the common good through restraints on individual misbehavior, self-sacrifice, and social engineering. The academy welcomes "immigrants," promotes educational achievement, and values citizen participation. The role of government is to protect the public from greedy politicians and corporations.

**Question**
A newly minted professor recognizes the inefficiency of government and even its total incompetence. He seeks to research this area to document his beliefs. He is offered a position at a private school in Yankeedom. Is this a good match?

*Answer*
Maybe not. The culture of the region derives from independent small towns and church congregations that were self-managed by citizens and worshippers. They trusted each other and their universities have faith and trust in the wisdom of the government.

## 2. New Netherland

Actually New York City, northern New Jersey, and Fairfield County, Connecticut, this is a multiethnic, multireligious, and highly materialistic culture. It evolved from Dutch settlers in an area dominated by the British in the 1700s. Its professors are global in perspective, supportive of diversity, and aggressive, perhaps, arrogant, in their desire to protect individual rights. They do not get together to discuss the common good. They demand that government do it without interfering with their individual rights and freedom to speak.

**Question**
Many citizens of New Netherlands support the individual right to abortion but not to carry guns. A professor with exactly the opposite view on both issues believes New York City would be a fertile area for academic research. Is that true?

*Answer*
Could be. If she pursues an agenda of opposition to abortion and research to justify no restrictions on gun ownership, her research may include confrontations both on and off the campus.

## 3. Tidewater

Approximating coastal Delaware to North Carolina, this fundamentally conservative region was shaped by country gentlemen, indentured servants, and slavery. It may be best described as a hierarchical society with control over property, religion, law, and government in the hands of those at the top of the economic and political power structure. Decent and capable people, perhaps, in the tradition of George Washington and Thomas Jefferson shaped the society. The colleges and universities value virtue and intelligence.

**Question**
A sociology professor attracted considerable attention pointing out failures of the federal government to provide sufficient economic support to urban areas. His research shows significant reduction in crime when residents in disadvantaged areas form their own community associations and use them to make improvements. He hopes to find a position at a university in the research triangle of North Carolina. Does that make sense?

*Answer*
You never know but the culture of the area is shaped by a belief that wealthy citizens had a natural propensity to make unselfish decisions to improve the lives of those less fortunate. Some difficulties might arise about the validity of his research or communications with students.

## 4. Deep South

Comprising an area from South Carolina to south Texas, this area is a stronghold of white supremacy, aristocratic order, privilege for the few, and limited democracy for the many. Its people support powerful leaders who resist increases in federal power and efforts to legislate environmental improvement, labor reform, consumer safety, and taxation of the wealthy.

**Question**
A doctoral candidate has offers from two private colleges, one in "Tidewater" and one in the "Deep South." A professor told him there is no real difference in their cultures. Is he right?

*Answer*
Not exactly. Both cultures restrict power to individuals at the top of the social and economic pyramid. Tidewater has a sense of obligation that encourages responsible behavior to individuals in the lower economic or social classes of society. In the Deep South, we see an attitude that society should serve those on top.

*South Florida—An Anomaly*

An anomaly is something that deviates from what is standard, normal, or expected. Woodard dismisses the lower part of Florida as "part of the Spanish

Caribbean." If a professor is looking here, she might also consider the Universidad de La Habana, Universidad Central de Venezuela, or Pontificia Universidad Católica de Puerto Rico.

## 5. Great Appalachia

A narrow band of counties crossing nineteen states from western Pennsylvania to the hill country of west Texas, the area was settled by subsequent waves of combative Irish, English, and Scottish immigrants. Although the term "Appalachia" is widely associated with rednecks and hillbillies, the area is more accurately described as protective of personal rights and resistant to outsiders. Professors here are suspicious of Tidewater aristocrats, Yankeedom community associations, and New Netherland intellectuals. They identify with Deep South antigovernment views and attack anything that threatens their rights or freedom. Strangers are not welcome.

### Question
A university in Greater Appalachia has three candidates for a professor job opening, all with good teaching and scholarship records. None were born in the United States. They come from Poland, Thailand, and Peru. Which one is most likely to appeal to the search committee?

*Answer*
No preference may be the answer. Once on the faculty, the reality may not be so pleasant for the successful candidate.

## 6. The Midlands

This oddly shaped collection of counties in fourteen states has two "head-quarters," the Midwest surrounding Iowa and the province of Ontario in Canada. The distinguishing characteristic of the "Midlands" is its founding by British Quakers who believed in basic human goodness. Citizens reject ethnic purity and strong oppressive religious or social ideology or regulation. Political views are moderate even as government is a minor intrusion in daily life. This area formed the quintessential North American middle class as viewed in song, story, and legend.

### Question
A faculty member wants to start an African American student society at a Midlands campus with 18 percent students of color. A colleague recommended waiting until she received tenure because of the possibility of a negative reaction from other professors. Is this good advice?

*Answer*
You never know for sure but The Midlands is generally a good area to advance causes that lead to inclusion and diversity. If the purpose is to reduce isolation, the effort could be widely viewed as being a positive service.

### 7. The Far West

A giant noncoastal land mass from the developed eastern and southern U.S. coasts, this area stops short of the Pacific coast while including western Canada. It represents lands historically protected from development by conservationists, climate, and geographic factors. Picture the cowboy to capture the culture where a rugged individualist confronts nature, isolation, and occasional incursions of unwelcome, distant urban interest. Everybody is equal and the individual can pursue any course he or she desires.

**Question**
A professor is at a Far West university that is experiencing an enrollment decline. She proposes an exchange program with colleges in Japan and Argentina to attract foreign students. Will the suggestion be well received?

*Answer*
Could be, but extra efforts will be needed to make it work as opposed to a location where such students have the potential for substantial community and cultural support.

### 8. The Left Coast

Consisting of land from south of San Francisco into British Columbia, these communities are within easy driving distance of the Pacific Ocean. Settled by either Yankeedom transplants who arrived by sea or Greater Appalachia migrants who arrived by covered wagon, the area is a blend of idealism, faith in good government, and social reform accompanied by self-exploration and a natural curiosity. The overriding cultural goal is to improve support systems that promote freedom of the individual in a long-term sustainable cultural and natural environment.

### 9. El Norte

A sprinkling of south Texas and southern California, a slice into New Mexico up into Colorado, and five border states of Mexico, this is a place dominated by Hispanic language, culture, and social norms. Residents fit a description as diligent, independent, self-sufficient, and adaptable. The area contains a high percentage of activists and starts many movements that affect other parts of North America.

### Question
A professor on a New Mexico campus in El Norte is promoting a cause to change the process of selecting federal judges. Is he likely to gain much support?

*Answer*
You never know, but the culture of El Norte often keeps itself out of touch with other parts of the nation and the academy.

### 10. New France

Consisting of Quebec in Canada and a small area around New Orleans, this is rarely a viable purgatory option.

### 11. First Nation

Comprising northern Canada and part of Alaska, this too is an isolated case.

## FINAL ADVICE

We are now nearing the end of our journey. If you are thinking about a permanent position, are you starting soon, underway, or languishing in purgatory? Whatever.

What do others think you should do? The *Chronicle of Higher Education* celebrated its fiftieth anniversary by taking stock of The Past and Future of Higher Education. As part of the project, it asked the question:

> What advice would you give a family member who wants to become an academic?

These are some slightly edited replies from readers:

> Don't! It's not a healthy or supportive career ... We care about students and teaching and our subject matter, but that cannot overcome the day-to-day dismal realities or put food on the table.

> To be an academic, you must work a minimum of 60 hours a week and spend vast amounts of time alone doing your research and writing, class preparation, and grading. Does that appeal to you? If not, think about another profession.

If they truly feel the passion to teach, they should embrace that passion to the fullest.

There are very few callings in life that are more maddening, more difficult, and more ultimately satisfying than being a professor. If you're called to answer big questions and inspire new thinkers, there's nowhere you'd rather be.

If you have a passion for teaching or research, being a professor is an ideal job. But be warned: Academic politics are intense and treacherous.

It's a tough road. Know what you're getting into. If you have a desire to teach, to have impact on lives, teach high school.

Do it. These are exciting times. The new generation of students is more open-minded, curious, and flexible than any other in recent history.

I advised my son that if he loved studying history so much that he was willing to live on a limited income and have his labor exploited for the next five to seven years, with no expectation that he would end up with a tenured position like mine, then he should go ahead and do it. He decided to pursue other options.

Go for it! Easy for a senior, tenured professor to say, perhaps.

Enter with your eyes open, your head in gear, your back strong, your spirit healthy, and your skin resilient.

## CONCLUSION

Now we are done. A siren song is an alluring utterance or appeal that makes you want to go somewhere or do something that may have bad results. Is that the allure of the academy? Or, eyes wide open and all circumstances weighed carefully, maybe you see the ability to do good for students and to advance the frontier of knowledge. If these are part of your value system, pursue it in harmony with many others who are working hard to reduce the number of our colleagues who are afraid to start, fearful of how their effort will turn out, or languishing in purgatory.

### The End
### Or is it just the beginning?

# Index

AACU general education outcomes, 151
AAUP conclusion on contingent faculty, 25
ABD downhill slope, 38
academentia, 133
academic appointments, 124
academic David, where is the?, 110
academic freedom, 168, 201
academic guild, modern, 22
academic purgatory, 7
academic purgatory, first level of, 37
academics purgatories, 202
academy, historical role of the, x
academy, rewards and recognition in the, 134
Plato's, 158
achieving tenure, success, 41
activities, faculty, 128
administration view on faculty duties, 29
adultism, 133
advance preparation for meetings, 143
advanced placement program, 133
alpha males and females, 60
alternative education, 133
alumni connections, weak, 119
American Nations and American Character, Colin Woodard, 201

analytic, 141
anchoring trap, 191
answers with high confidence, 88
answers, right, wrong, with high confidence, 88
applied and integrative learning, 151
appointments, academic, 124
apprentice, 20
argumentation, 153
assertiveness, 141
assessing need for faculty, 30
assessment, 133
assessment of faculty by deans, by peers, 32
assignments, common, 101

backup plan for tenure, 200
backup style, 142
Bandwagon effect, 189
baseball economics, 31
Beaumont university "story", 55
bias, thin slice of, among professionals, 192
blended learning, 133
books reviews, professional, 132
books, professional, 131
Bozo explosion in the academy, 68
business mathematics class, 157

209

campus attitudes on freedom of
    speech, 173
can learning be fun?, 54
candidate, qualified, 123
cats and confidence, 67
causation and correlation, 64
CBS Moneywatch, 14
Chaffey college, incident at, 35
chair of department, 140
challenges to what we believe, 157
changing condition for professors, xii
Chicago cubs, great professors, 49
childhood dreams, 104
Chinese meritocracy, 158
choice of a college or university, 111
classroom results, 88
    decorum in the, 102
    flipped, 161
    honorific gestures in the, 103
    Ian Lamont on the, 156,
    unexpected, cursive in the, 94
college and career ready—student
    version, 91
    professor version, 92
college committees, list of, 33
college or university, choice of, 111
committees, list of in colleges, 33
common assignments, 101
common good, 201
common lecture, 101
common textbook, 100
communications style, 144
compelling visions, 99
compensation for contingent faculty, 24
completing the dissertation, 196
components of online course, 159
computer based learning, 133
conference, proceedings, 132
confidence and cats, 67
confirmation bias, 189
connections, role of, weak, 118
connectors, mavens, and salesmen, 119
context of "prison", 53
contingent faculty, 23
    AAUP conclusion, 25
    faculty views on, 26
    stakeholder views, 26
contradiction for professors, 51
controversial messages and academic
    freedom, 173
cooperative education, 133
correlation and causation, 64
course grades and academic freedom, 172
course, problems with, 82
courses, in-person, hybrid, and
    online, 159
creationism taught in public
    schools, 182
curse disguised as a wish, 16
cursive in the classroom, 94
cursive, is it obsolete?, 93

Dante's journey to paradise, 4
David and Goliath, 110
David in the classroom, in career
    decisions, 112
deans, how do they assess faculty?, 32
decision-making style, 144
decorum in the classroom, 102
deep south, 204
deficient love, 188
déformation professionnelle, 190
degree completion, obstacles to, 38
degree completion, time to, 37
deliberative decision-making style, 145
department chair, 140
despair by the candidate, 38
discontinuance for educational
    reasons, 178
discussions of honesty and ethics, 89
dismal science, tenured faculty?, 29
dismissal for cause, 177
dissertation, finishing the, 39
    completing and publishing, 196
doctoral programs, tuition/fees, 40
door to reform, opening a, 57
Downhill ABD slope, 38
dreams, enabling of others, 104
driver, 141
due process, 178

economic view of full-time faculty, 31
El Norte, 206
election result, can a professor predict?, 65
eleven academic purgatories, 202
encounter over a syllabus, 79
endowment effect, 189
enhance learning with humor, 82
epic struggles in North America, 201
ethics and honesty, discussions of, 89
evaluating teaching, scholarship and service, 128–132
evidence, known and silent, 63
expectations for professors, 46
expertise and knowledge, 61
expressive, 141

faculty activities, 128
faculty assessment, how do deans and peers do it?, 32
faculty duties, administration view, 29
faculty evaluations, misconceptions of, 135
faculty views on contingent faculty, 26
faculty, contingent, 23
faculty, contingent, compensation for, 24
faculty, full-time, 22
faculty, life on the, 97
failure of traditional methods, 157
father on a train, 106
financial exigency, 178
finishing the dissertation, 39
first level of academic purgatory, 37
first nation, 207
flipped classroom, 161
freedom of speech, campus attitudes on, 173
Freud on thin slices, 194
full-time faculty, 22
  economic view of, 31
fun, can learning be?, 54
fun, students have when engaged, 88

general education, 100
  outcomes, AACU, Lemann, 151

general interest publications, 131
genius professors, 60
Goliath in the classroom, during the dissertation, on the tenure track, in the hiring process, in a tenured status, 110
great Appalachia, 205
great professors, Chicago cubs, secret of, 47–50
great teachers dispel misconceptions, 53
guild medieval, 20

hands-off manager, 142
hands-on manager, 142
Hartwick or Harvard?, 112, 152
Harvard or Hartwick?, 112
hell after purgatory, 8
help or support, x
hidden traps, 188
hiring process revealed, role of luck, 116
  official and unofficial, 118
historical role of the academy, x
history of tenure, 177
honesty and even ethics, discussions of, 89
honorific gestures in the classroom, 103
how expensive is the Ph.D?, 40
humor to enhance learning, 82
humor, professor, 60
hybrid course, consider if you will, 161
hybrid, online, and in-person courses, 159

Ian Lamont on the classroom, 156
idiosyncrasies of search committees, 120
illusionary superiority, 60
in-person, hybrid, and online courses, 159
incident at Chaffey College, 35
individual liberty, 201
inept professors, 60
information acquisition, 152
innovation, speaking up, 73

integrative and applied learning, 151
integrative learning, 133
intellectual and practical skills, 151
intellectual communicator, 144
interpretation of written meaning, 152
inward communicator, 144
irrational escalation, 190
is tenure a litmus test?, 180

job market, post Ph.D, 40
journals, scholarly, 131
journey to paradise, professor's, 6
journeyman, 20
justification for tenure, 176

Kentucky derby winner, pick the, 84
knowing, mistake of, 63
knowledge and expertise, 61
known silent evidence, 63

last lecture, 104
learning management system
    (LMS) 160
learning, integrative and applied, 151
lecture, common, 101
  the last, 104
Lemann, Nicholas on general
    education, 151
liberal arts, 150
liberal arts tradition, x
life on the faculty, 97
life, stages of, 4
limbo, misplaced, peer review is the
    path out of, 196–197
litmus test is tenure a?, 180
living classroom, 85
LMS, (learning management
    system) 160
love, perverted and deficient, 188

management style, 142
master craftsman, 20
Mavens, salesmen, and connectors, 119
McDonald's, what do you know
    about?, 85

medieval guild, 20
medieval university, 21, 133, 158
meetings, purpose of, advance
    preparation for, 143
misconceptions, great teachers
    dispel, 53
  of faculty evaluations, 135
misplaced limbo, 196
mistake of knowing, 63
misunderstanding by the candidate, 38
modern academic guild, 22
moneywatch, CBS, 14
mount purgatory, 188
movie, the trench, 37

Naatus, professor Mary Kate, 104
need for faculty, assessing, 30
need to know, new instructors, 75
New France, 207
new instructors need to know, 75
New Netherland, 203
North America, epic struggles in, 201
numerical literacy, 152

obsessions and subtleties, 133
obsolete, is cursive?, 93
obstacles to degree completion, 38
official hiring process, 118
online course, components of, 159
online courses, quiz on knowledge of,
    statistics for, 162
online, in-person, and hybrid
    courses, 159
opening a door to reform, 57
outcomes, AACU general
    education, 151
outward communicator, 144
overconfident, we tend to be, 88

paradise, Dante's journey to, 4
part timers in the hallways, 35
path out of limbo, peer review, 197
peer review is the path out of
    limbo, 197
peers how do they assess faculty?, 32

# Index

personal and social responsibility, 151
personal perspectives, 153
perverted love, 188
Ph.D, how expensive?, 40
Plato's academy, 158
politics of tenure, 199
post Ph.D job market, 40
practices, style, and situations in teaching, 72
prison, context of, 53
problems with the course, 82
proceedings, conference, 132
professional books, trade journals, working papers, 131
professional working papers, 132
professionals, bias among, 193
professor predict an election result?, 65
professor version, college and career ready, 92
professor, what is a?, 11
   humor, 60
professor's journey to paradise, 6
professorial "intelligence", 47
professors, changing condition for, xii
   contradiction for, 51
   "genius", 60
   inept, 60
   our expectations for, 46
   "profess", 46
   what do schools want from?, 117
professorships, the temptation of, 187
public speech and academic freedom, 171
publications, general interest, 131
publish or perish, 22
publishing your dissertation, 198
purgatories, eleven academic, 202
purgatory, in Christian theology, 5
   academic, 7
   hell after, 8
   multiple levels of, 202
purpose of meetings, 143
pursuit of tenure, 197

qualified candidate, 123
quiz on knowledge of online courses, 162

ranking scholarship, 131
reduction of teaching load, 128
republican, is a litmus test?, 181
responsiveness, 141
rewards and recognition in the academy, 134
right answers, 88
rollins College, 155
rules, sometimes not liked by students, 88

salesmen, connectors, and mavens, 119
scholarly journals, 131
scholarship, evaluating, ranking, 130
search committees, idiosyncrasies of, 120
secret of great professors, 50
service, evaluating, 132
silent evidence, 63
situations, style, and practices in teaching, 72
skills, intellectual and practical, 151
slides, tips for using, 83
SNHU (Southern New Hampshire University) 151
social and personal responsibility, 151
social style, 141
Southern New Hampshire University (SNHU) 151
speaking up innovation, 73
speedy decision-making style, 145
Spitzer, Eliot, 13
stages of life, 4
standard teaching load, 128
statistics for online classes, 164
status quo trap, 191
sticky does not stand alone, 52
sticky stories, 50
student evaluations, 129

student version, college and career ready, 91
students, sometimes do not like rules, 88
students, when engaged have fun, 88
style, situations, and practices in teaching, 72
subtleties and obsessions, 133
success achieving tenure, 41
success, six key attributes, 50
successful department chair, 145
Sunk cost trap, 191
superiority, illusionary, 60
supportive, 141
swimming against the current, 36
syllabus, encounter over, 79

task manager, 142
teaching load, reduction of, standard, 128
teaching, evaluating, 128
teaching, style, situations, and practices in, 72
team manager, 142
tenure, success achieving, 41
tenure, what is?, 176
   backup plan for, 200
   policy change, 2016 Wisconsin, 178
   politics of, 199
   pursuit of, 197
tenured faculty, a dismal science?, 29
textbook, common, 100
the Far West, 206
the Left Coast, 206
the Midlands, 205
the temptation of professorships, 187
thin slice of bias, 192
thin slices, Freud on, 194
thinking in time, 153
tidewater, 203
time limit to finish, 15
time to degree completion, 37
tips for using slides, 83

traditional methods, failure of, 157
train, father on a, 106
traps, hidden, 188
trench, the movie, 37
tuition/fees in selected doctoral programs, 40
two-way communicator, 144

unexpected classroom results, 88
university, medieval, 21, 158
   rights, 169
unknown silent evidence, 63
unofficial hiring process, 118

value over replacement player (VORP) economics, 31
versatility, 141
vision, where is the?, 102
visions, compelling, 99
visual language, 153
VORP economics, 31

weak alumni connections, 119
weaknesses of management styles, 143
Whackademia, 134
what are our expectations for professors?, 46
what is tenure?, 176
what we believe, challenges to, 157
where is the vision?, 102
winner of the Kentucky Derby, pick the, 84
Wisconsin's, 2016 tenure policy change, 178
wish disguised as a curse, 16
Wonkish, praise to be called?, 14
Woodard Colin, American Nations and American Character, 201
working papers, Professionals, 132
wrong answers, 88

Yankeedom, 202

# About the Author

**Jack Hampton** is a professor of business at St. Peter's University in New Jersey. In a faculty capacity, he was an endowed chair holder (twice), department chair, director of a division of research, and director of graduate business programs. He was the dean of the schools of business at Seton Hall and Connecticut State universities and the evening school at St. Peter's. He was provost of the College of Insurance and SUNY Maritime College, both in New York City.

Jack is the author of more than thirty books, two of which were recognized with innovation awards (2008 and 2012). The latter was also selected by the American Library Association as one of three outstanding business reference books. His earlier book on higher education, *Culture, Intricacies, and Obsessions in Academia: Why Colleges and Universities are Struggling to Deliver the Goods*, was published by Rowman and Littlefield in 2017.

www.ingramcontent.com/pod-product-compliance
Lightning Source LLC
Chambersburg PA
CBHW020830020526
44115CB00029B/72